YOUNG MEN IN DETENTION CENTRES

INTERNATIONAL LIBRARY OF SOCIOLOGY AND SOCIAL RECONSTRUCTION

Founded by Karl Mannheim

Editor: W. J. H. Sprott

A catalogue of the books available in the INTERNATIONAL LIBRARY OF SOCIOLOGY AND SOCIAL RECONSTRUCTION, and new books in preparation for the Library, will be found at the end of this volume.

YOUNG MEN
IN
DETENTION CENTRES

by

ANNE B. DUNLOP

and

SARAH McCABE

LONDON
ROUTLEDGE & KEGAN PAUL
NEW YORK: THE HUMANITIES PRESS

First published 1965
by Routledge & Kegan Paul Limited
Broadway House, 68-74 Carter Lane
London, E.C.4

Printed in Great Britain
by Charles Birchall & Sons Limited
Liverpool and London

CONTENTS

Preface   *page* vii

Introduction   ix

1. The Origin and Development of the Detention Centres
    in England   1

2. The Background and Criminal History of the Young
    Men Who Were the Subject of this Study   22

3. The First Interview   50

4. The Young Men as They Appeared to the Officers at
    the Centres   75

5. The Second Interview   95

6. A Limited Follow-up of These Young Men After Their
    Discharge   125

7. Summary and Conclusions   133

Appendices

Two Case Studies   140

Forms used in the Enquiry   146

The Detention Centre Rules   155

Index   175

PREFACE

THE authors of this study are grateful to the Home Office and the Social Studies Board of the University of Oxford for the support that was given to them throughout the course of this work.

They are indebted in particular to Mr. T. S. Lodge, Statistical Adviser and Director of Research at the Home Office, for his support of the research plan and for the helpful criticism he offered as it developed.

Mr. A. W. Peterson, who was then Chairman of the Prison Commission, provided all the facilities for the research to be carried out and helped greatly with his advice and criticism while the report was being compiled.

Throughout the work, the wardens and prison officers at Werrington and Aylesbury Detention Centres showed great kindness and forbearance with the inroads that were made upon their time and with the questions that were asked of them. The officers at Werrington also took part in a long group discussion. The Wardens and deputy-wardens of the other detention centres in England and of the Scottish detention centre at Perth gave much information and advice. So too did the officers responsible for running the senior Attendance Centre at Manchester.

For advice and criticism the authors rested securely upon the support of Dr. M. Grünhut, under whose general direction the work was done.

Last of all, to the young men at Werrington and Aylesbury Detention Centres who answered as best they could the many questions that were asked of them, the authors owe the widening of their own horizons and a deeper understanding of some of the penal problems of the present time.

ANNE B. DUNLOP
SARAH McCABE

INTRODUCTION

ONE of the most characteristic patterns of recent English penal policy is the rapid spread of detention centres. Any new development of this kind makes it necessary to examine the possible effects of the new measures and to test by reliable methods of criminological research whether the new forms of treatment have led to the desired results. This is particularly so with methods of treatment for which there is no previous parallel. It was from such a proposition that the present study of senior detention centres was undertaken.

From the beginning of this penal experiment, the Home Office and the Prison Commission have facilitated research into its results. A study of the first 434 boys received into the first junior centre at Campsfield House and the first 144 young men received into the senior centre at Blantyre House was published in the *British Journal of Delinquency* in 1960.[1] This showed that more than one in every three of the young men committed to the senior centre did not get on well with their families, had a record of instability of employment or actual unemployment and made no attempt to use their considerable leisure effectively. The reconviction rate of this senior group within a period of two years after their release from detention was 36.1 per cent. for those released into civilian life and 43.5 per cent. for those who were returned to the army or were conscripted soon after their release.

This study of a senior centre was based entirely on records available at the centre and on evidence of reconvictions obtained from the police and the military authorities.

In view of the extension of the use of detention centres proposed in the White Paper on Penal Practice in a Changing Society it was decided to make some further attempt to evaluate the work

[1] *British Journal of Delinquency* (later *British Journal of Criminology*) vol. 10, 1960, p. 177.

of detention centres for the age-group seventeen to twenty-one and to see what effect this form of punishment had upon those who were subjected to it.

The great difficulty in every form of criminological research into penal treatment is to find the right criterion for success or failure. Reconviction rates will always be an important starting point but their limitations as a reliable criterion are obvious. It might be desirable for criminological purposes to supplement them by more composite studies as a test of social adjustment. Even so it would be extremely difficult to isolate the treatment factor as a possible cause of success or failure. This is particularly so when one has to deal with young people whose modes of life are bound to undergo considerable changes. It was for these reasons that the authors wished to concentrate on the personal response of the young men to the treatment awarded to them. For such attitude research a wide range of instruments appears to be available, from the casual observations by prison officers to standardized methods of interviews in depth and projective tests. From a critical point of view, all these methods have their limitations. All the evidence remains in need of interpretation and in addition the result of the attitude research is inevitably coloured by the test situation. These impediments are particularly strong in the case of attitude studies of men in prison. Any direct or indirect answer is affected, if not by wilful deceit, at least by a conscious or unconscious desire to please and to satisfy what are thought to be the needs of the interrogator.

Faced with these difficulties, the authors, in conjunction with the Prison Commission, decided to steer a middle course and to concentrate on methodically prepared interviews on the lines used in modern social casework. After all, this is the sort of information that would be available, in favourable circumstances, to sentencing courts. It goes without saying that the interviews themselves and the appraisal of the results had to have regard to the personal circumstances of the offenders and the conditions under which they lived while they were in the detention centre.

Throughout the whole study the offenders between the ages of seventeen and twenty-one have deliberately been called young men. Those who are committed to approved schools are called 'boys', those undergoing borstal training are called 'lads'—a name more justified by tradition than aptness. Those sent to senior detention centres have already taken their place as adults, in work and in life in the community. If the behaviour which led to their sentence of detention often showed considerable immaturity, it is all the more necessary to appeal to their sense of adulthood.

The two centres chosen for the experiment were Werrington House, near Stoke-on-Trent, and Aylesbury Centre, which was adapted for use as a detention centre after the girl's borstal and women's prison had been removed elsewhere.

The two research workers visited each centre once each week and interviewed each of the men who had been received in the centre during the preceding seven days. The interview was conducted in private, each interviewer having a separate room in which she talked to one man at a time. A questionnaire had been prepared and the purpose of this was carefully explained to the men. Emphasis was laid on the unofficial nature of the interview. The information given would not be disclosed to the warden or any of the prison officers and no publication would reveal the identity of the offender. The questions were then put to the men generally in the set order of the questionnaire. If they were unable to understand any question, it was carefully explained to them. When a man was anxious to talk at the beginning of the interview, it was not thought to be advisable to stop him but to direct his flow of talk along the lines of the questionnaire where this was possible. This situation arose whenever a man was very disturbed about his detention and the reaction of his family to it. Sometimes it was not possible to put the questions in proper sequence because the offender was so anxious to justify himself that he evaded questions that might implicate him and returned again and again to points where his own innocence and good behaviour were made clear. Difficulties were also encountered with men of low intelligence who could not always be made to understand the point of the questions.

The next stage in the research was to obtain from the prison officers reports on the attitude and the behaviour of the men who had been interviewed at the beginning of their sentence. The men were interviewed for a second time between two and eight days before their discharge. The same interviewer saw him for the second time and asked a series of questions that resembled those that had been put at the first interview. There were some additions to the questionnaire and some of the questions were deliberately disguised so that the men should not give a mechanical repetition of an answer consciously or unconsciously recalled.

The last stage in the investigation was the issue of follow-up letters to each of the men who had been interviewed. They had already been asked if they would agree to have a letter written to them asking for details of employment and general resettlement after discharge. Not one man refused this request. The letters themselves were issued three or four months after each man's discharge. A stamped and addressed envelope was enclosed with each so that there was no difficulty or expense involved for the men.

To complete the study and provide the background for the report upon it, the two research workers visited each of the senior detention centres in operation in England. The Scottish detention centre at Perth was also visited.

In order to make some comparison between detention and other measures available to the courts, one of the research workers also visited the senior attendance centre at Manchester.

Before making an assessment of the results of the interviews, the research workers built up a case history of each man they had interviewed. The material was obtained from the files at the detention centre which held reports from the police, the school, the probation officer and so on.

Each interviewer then interpreted the information she had obtained and assessed the attitude of each offender towards his offence and his detention. All this information was then pooled and the report written in collaboration.

CHAPTER ONE

THE ORIGIN AND DEVELOPMENT OF THE DETENTION CENTRES IN ENGLAND

THE Criminal Justice Act of 1948 abolished the sentence of corporal punishment and limited the power of the courts to commit to prison offenders under the age of twenty-one. These reductions in the armoury of the criminal courts were made good by the sentence of detention in a detention centre and, to some extent, by orders to attend an attendance centre. Although the Act of 1948 had its origins in the Criminal Justice Bill of 1938, which had reached an advanced stage in its passage through Parliament before it was put aside in 1939 owing to preparations for war, there were, in fact, no provisions for the setting up of detention centres in this earlier Bill. It was thought at that time that the proper treatment of young offenders could be accomplished by residential hostels (Howard Houses) and attendance centres.

In 1947, the Home Secretary, Mr. Chuter Ede, introducing the new Criminal Justice Bill, explained the function of a detention centre :

'It provides for the young offender for whom a fine or probation order would be inadequate, but who does not require the prolonged period of training which is given by an approved school or a borstal institution. There is a type of offender to whom it seems necessary to give a short but sharp reminder that he is getting into ways that will inevitably lead him into disaster.'[1]

During the debate that followed, there was little discussion of the purpose and methods of the new institutions;[2] attention was

[1]*Hansard* 1947-48, Vol. 444, c. 2138.

[2]Sir George Benson pointed out this failure to look deeply into the new proposals for detention in a detention centre and corrective training. He remarked that no one had thought of asking what they would be like and how they would run. Despite this, little was said later in the Commons debate. *Hansard* 1947-48, Vol. 444, c. 2286.

concentrated on the possibility of the restriction or abolition of the death sentence, on the abolition of corporal punishment and the treatment of younger offenders, especially in approved schools. When the Bill reached the Lords it was left to Lord Templewood, who as Sir Samuel Hoare had been responsible for the earlier proposals, to ask whether detention in a detention centre would, in fact, be anything else but imprisonment. In this he was speaking for the Magistrates Association as well as for himself, and, on their behalf also, he suggested that the attendance centres and residential hostels which had been outlined in the 1938 Bill would be sufficient to provide 'a quick, sharp punishment of the kind that would not mean a break, or a serious break in the young offender's life'.[3] He agreed, however, to await events and see how the new penal experiment turned out.

As it finally reached the statute book, the new measure defined within broad limits the kind of offender for whom a sentence of detention was designed. First, the offence committed must be one for which a term of imprisonment could have been imposed. (This is a very wide definition since nearly every statutory offence carries, as its maximum penalty, a sentence of imprisonment. Wilful damage, offences of drunkenness and disorderly behaviour, all forms and degrees of larceny are punishable in this way.) Second, the offender must be over fourteen and under twenty-one years of age. Third, no offender who has served a borstal or prison sentence may be sentenced to detention. Fourth, no offender may be so sentenced unless the court has considered every other method of dealing with him and has found them inappropriate. For offenders who satisfied these four requirements the Prison Commission prepared to establish the new centres. In doing so they made the usual distinction between offenders under the age of seventeen who fall within the jurisdiction of the juvenile courts, and those between the ages of seventeen and twenty-one who are subjected to the rigour of adult criminal procedure. Since the increase in crime in 1951 was particularly marked in the age-group fourteen to seventeen, they decided to try out the new penal institution by opening a junior centre.

In 1952 the first detention centre for boys of fourteen and under seventeen years of age was opened at Campsfield House, Kidlington near Oxford. At first the regime was exacting and

[3] *Hansard,* Lords Debates, vol. 156, June 1948, c. 297.

severe so that criticisms were immediately levelled at this institution on the grounds that it was harsh, unconstructive and ill-adapted to further the aims of any treatment prescribed by a juvenile court. Such views, common among social workers and social scientists, found expression in this forthright denial of its usefulness.

So far as I understand this so-called shock treatment, it depends upon the denial of human contact between the boy and members of the staff; in my judgement it runs counter to all the most hopeful developments in the treatment of delinquency. This, after all, is what the boy expects of society and in the Detention Centre, society duly obliges by providing it; the Centre offers no challenge to the boy and seeks no response from him other than obedience.[4]

The Prison Commissioners Report of 1952 acknowledged the existence of such criticism, but emphasized once more that the first aim of the new institutions was deterrence.[5] Nevertheless, some changes were made in the severity of the regime and 'there was a noticeable "mellowing" in the atmosphere of the Centre'.[6] Probation officers, however, and social workers generally, still withheld approval from a penal measure that was enforceable by juvenile courts, that was too short for real treatment, and that had no satisfactory provisions for after-care. It is interesting to speculate whether criticism would have been so violent or so sustained if the first detention centre to be opened had been a senior centre for offenders over the age of seventeen.

Despite the volume of criticism, a second centre, this time for older offenders, was opened at Blantyre House, near Goudhurst in August 1954, and the courts made immediate use of the new facility. Committals to both centres were, however, rather haphazard until a study of the results of the sentence was published. This showed that, in terms of reconvictions, at least, the effect of detention upon ex-approved schoolboys and upon those whose criminal behaviour was long-lasting was not good enough to justify its continued use in such cases.[7]

[4]Donald Ford, *The Delinquent Child in the Community,* Constable, 1957, p. 56.
[5]Report of the Prison Commissioners for 1952. Cm. 8984 p. 91.
[6]Report of the Prison Commissioners for 1954. Cm. 9547 p. 87.
[7]M. Grünhut. 'Juvenile Delinquents under Punitive Detention,' *British Journal of Delinquency,* vol. 5, 1955, p. 191.

On the basis of this study and in answer to the expressions of doubt about the usefulness of detention, efforts were made to ensure a better selection of offenders for this form of treatment. A Home Office circular gave advice to courts about the kind of offender most likely to respond to detention. Meanwhile, public anxiety about the growing criminality of the age-group seventeen to twenty-one led judges and magistrates to press for the opening of more senior centres. A second one was, therefore, opened early in 1957. This was at Werrington in Staffordshire and it received offenders from the northern and midland courts. Accommodation was now available for 142 young men between the ages of seventeen and twenty-one and 600 offenders could be received each year. This was not yet enough to provide an alternative to all sentences of imprisonment for men of this age-group. Moreover, the whole question of the treatment of offenders committed to penal institutions for short terms had been referred to the Advisory Council on the Treatment of Offenders and their Report on the Alternatives to Short Term Imprisonment[8] was expected to indicate the trend of informed opinion at that time. The Advisory Council had considered what steps could be taken to reduce the number of committals to prison for periods of less than six months; its recommendations included the imposition of heavier fines, the use of supervision when time was allowed for payment, the provision of attendance centres for offenders over seventeen and the speedy implementation of the provisions of the Criminal Justice Act for remand centres. There was no mention of detention in a detention centre although the senior centre at Goudhurst had been open for more than a year when the committee of the Council began its enquiries. The senior attendance centre recommended by the Advisory Council was opened in Manchester in 1958. This, unlike the junior centre, was administered and staffed by the Prison Commission. Obviously, however, official policy was moving towards a solution of the problem of the treatment of young offenders that would make extensive use of senior detention centres. In 1958 the Advisory Council was asked to comment on specific proposals for the sentencing of offenders under the age of twenty-one. These were, first, that sentences under six months should be served in detention centres; second, that sentences between six months and two years should be indeter-

[8]H.M.S.O. 1957.

minate and be served in borstal type institutions and third, that imprisonment should be available as a sentence for offenders under twenty-one only when a term of three years or more was thought to be appropriate.

Before the Council examined these proposals in detail, the Home Secretary published, early in 1959, the White Paper on 'Penal Practice in a Changing Society'.[9] This contained the proposals for the treatment of young offenders which are outlined above. The White Paper, however, attracted little attention and what reaction there was, was generally favourable.[10] The seal of approval was finally set upon this new venture in penal policy and administration by the full Report of the Advisory Council which said 'the deficiencies of short sentences of imprisonment have, to a great extent, been overcome in detention centres'.[11] At the same time, the Report stressed that 'the penal treatment of young offenders should be primarily remedial' and claimed that 'the system has already shown some flexibility in expanding the original conception of a regime based primarily on deterrence to include elements of positive training'.[12]

With this powerful backing and little adverse public comment, a new Criminal Justice Bill was introduced early in 1960 containing provisions for the ultimate replacement of the majority of prison sentences for offenders under the age of twenty-one by sentences of detention, and the establishment of a system based on a shortened borstal sentence for periods between six months and two years. Sentences of over three years remained available for grave crimes and for offenders for whom such long terms of imprisonment seemed necessary. There was little alteration in these provisions during the passage of the Bill through both Houses.

The debate outside Parliament centred round the possible differences between detention centres and prisons. It had been demonstrated that detention in a detention centre served a useful purpose for certain selected offenders.[13] It was argued that it

[9]'Penal Practice in a Changing Society,' White Paper, Cm. 645, 1959.

[10]Report of the Advisory Council on the Treatment of Offenders, H.M.S.O. 1959, p. 3. para. 3.

[11]Report of the Advisory Council on the Treatment of Offenders, H.M.S.O. 1959, para. 24.

[12]ibid, para. 7, 27, 31.

[13]M. Grünhut, Juvenile Delinquents under Punitive Detention,' *British Journal of Delinquency*, vol. 5, 1955.

5

could not, with continued good effect, be used indiscriminately. A second objection was to the length of sentences of detention. Sentences of three months and six months were not easy to integrate within one centre; under the Bill it would be possible, by a system of cumulative sentences and orders, for an offender to be sentenced to nine months' detention. In contrast, the Report of the Scottish Advisory Council on the Treatment of Offenders recommended a uniform sentence of three months.[14]

The provisions for statutory after-care—a long-felt need— received a whole-hearted welcome, although there was some discussion about the treatment of those who broke the conditions of their supervision after release. The provisions of the 1961 Act involve the return of the offender to the centre for the unexpired portion of his sentence or for fourteen days, whichever is the greater. There does not seem to be any sound alternative to this solution but it will be noted that detention centres will, when the provisions come into effect, be able to receive some offenders for periods of fourteen days in addition to those sentenced for periods of three to nine months. It remains to be seen whether the new provisions for after-care will out-weigh the disadvantages of large variations in the lengths of sentence.

Since detention centres, borstal institutions and prisons are now to be used as alternative forms of penal institutions for young offenders under the age of twenty-one some comparison of the recent committals to each of those types of institution might prove useful.

Table 1[15] shows the offences for which young men were sentenced to detention, to borstal and to prison for the years 1959, 1960 and 1961. There is a marked difference between the kind of offences committed by those who were sentenced to borstal and those who were sentenced to detention and imprisonment. Clearly the longer training provided by borstal institutions is thought to be more suitable for dishonest offenders while those found guilty of offences of violence are expected to be amenable to the deterrent regimes of detention centres and prisons.

The similarity between the type of offence committed by those

[14]Report of the Scottish Advisory Council on the Treatment of Offenders, H.M.S.O., Edinburgh, 1960.
[15]Compiled from figures taken from the Report of the Prison Commissioners for 1960.

Table 1: *Analysis of the offences of offenders sentenced to detention, borstal training and imprisonment in the years 1959 1960 and 1961*

	Detention Centres						Borstal Institutions						Prisons					
	1959 No.	%	1960 No.	%	1961 No.	%	1959 No.	%	1960 No.	%	1961 No.	%	1959 No.	%	1960 No.	%	1961 No.	%
Offences of dishonesty	334	0	304	45	828	50	2,599	85	2,842	82	2,866	80	1,052	42	1,162	44	1,066	42
Offences of violence	125	17	112	17	244	14	235	8	326	9	301	8	537	22	609	22	544	22
Motoring offences	91	14	166	25	388	22	77	2	63	2	182	5	355	14	449	17	402	15
Other offences	138	19	83	13	216	14	151	5	245	7	239	7	554	22	451	17	533	21
All	688	100	665	100	1,676	100	3,062	100	3,476	100	3,588	100	2,498	100	2,671	100	2,545	100

Table 2: *Length of sentence, analysed by the offence committed, of male offenders aged 17-21 sentenced to imprisonment in 1960*

	Sentences under 3 months		Sentences between 3 and 6 months		Sentences between 6 and 12 months		Sentences over 12 months	
	No.	%	No.	%	No.	%	No.	%
Offences of violence *	215	18	159	23	62	16	80	22
Sexual offences	8	—	19	3	24	6	42	11
Offences of dishonesty	473	39	312	45	296	76	243	67
Offences of taking and driving away	209	17	103	15	4	1	1	—
Other motoring offences	77	6	54	8	1	—	—	—
All other offences	243	20	43	6	3	1	—	—
	1,225	100	690	100	390	100	336	100

* Offences of violence include all assaults, indictable and otherwise, actual, grievous bodily harm and murder.

8

Table 3: *Previous convictions of male offenders aged 17-21 sentenced to borstal training, imprisonment and detention in a detention centre in 1959, 1960 and 1961*

No. of previous convictions	Senior Detention Centres Percentage of committals			Borstal Institutions Percentage of committals			Prisons Percentage of committals		
	1959	1960	1961	1959	1960	1961	1959	1960	1961
Nil	16 ⎫	14 ⎫	13 ⎫	6 ⎫	5 ⎫	5 ⎫	26 ⎫	12 ⎫	14 ⎫
One	25 ⎬66	24 ⎬61	14 ⎬41	13 ⎬38	13 ⎬36	12 ⎬34	13 ⎬53	12 ⎬39	11 ⎬36
Two	25 ⎭	23 ⎭	14 ⎭	19 ⎭	18 ⎭	17 ⎭	14 ⎭	15 ⎭	11 ⎭
Three	15	16	13	19	20	20	12	13	14
Four	9	10	11	16	17	16	10	14	13
Five and over	10	13	35	27	27	30	25	34	37
All	100	100	100	100	100	100	100	100	100

9

who are sent to detention centres and those who are committed to prison is one argument in favour of merging the populations of prisons and detention centres. This is envisaged by the authorities as a practical proposition for sentences between three and six months. Longer sentences are to be served in borstal institutions or in prisons.

Table 2[16] shows the length of the prison sentences of young men between seventeen and twenty-one committed to prison in 1960. It is noticeable that the proportion of dishonest offenders increases among those with a longer period of sentence. The majority of prison sentences under three months are given for offences of violence, motoring offences, malicious damage, drunkenness and other contraventions of the social code which may not be serious in character.

A further basis of comparison for these three penal methods is to be found in the records of the previous offences of those who were committed to them. Table 3[17] shows for 1959, 1960 and 1961 the previous proved offences of offenders sent to each kind of institution.

Committals to detention centres have, until 1961, shown a consistent pattern of offenders sentenced to detention at an early stage in their criminal careers. Among those sentenced to imprisonment an increasing proportion has a long record of previous offences. In 1961, however, among those sentenced to detention, nearly one-half had previously been found guilty of four or more offences. This change in the character of the detention centre population may be the result of the sentencing policy of the courts or the availability of more detention centre places in 1961. It may also be due to a general change in the kind of offender who is brought before the courts. Whatever the reason for this significant increase in the number and proportion of criminally sophisticated offenders now being committed to detention centres, its effect on the detention centre system must be considerable.

The three penal institutions for young men may be compared by considering the reconviction rates of those who were committed

[16]Compiled from figures taken from the Report of the Prison Comissioners for 1960. Table D11.

[17]Table compiled from figures given in the Report of the Prison Commissioners for 1959 and 1960—Appendix I, Table III; Tables D9, D11 and D15, pp. 170, 174 and 182.

to them. Such a simple test of effectiveness is not fully reliable since borstal trainees enjoy a period of statutory after-care that should reduce their reconviction rate for the period immediately following their release and the reconviction figures for those sentenced to imprisonment are not always adequately reported and recorded. Nevertheless, the reconviction rates show one more difference between these penal methods. Table 4[18] shows the percentage of men reconvicted within three years of their release from senior detention centres, borstals and imprisonment in young prisoners' centres.

Table 4: Number of males discharged during 1957, and percentage reconvicted by the end of 1960

	Discharged during 1957	Reconvicted by end of 1960
Senior detention centre	498	55%
Borstals	1,703	65%
Young prisoners' centres	771	50%

The difference in reconviction rates shown here need not indicate a greater efficiency in training methods or power of deterrence in prisons and detention centres, but only that they have so far received the less difficult offenders.

The situation and physical characteristics of the centres

When this enquiry was begun there were two senior centres, one at Goudhurst in Kent and one at Werrington in Staffordshire. Since then four more have been opened, and several more are planned.[19]

Blantyre House detention centre, which was the first senior centre to be opened, lies a mile or two from Goudhurst village in Kent. The buildings, originally a children's home, surround a parade ground which can be flood-lit at night for evening games.

[18]Figures compiled from Report of the Prison Commissioners for 1960, pp. 190, 191 and 196. This is a very rough comparison but reliable enough to indicate the general extent of the difference in results.

[19]'Penal Practice in a Changing Society,' H.M.S.O. Cm. 645, 1959. (This was the position at the time this report was written. Several more Centres have since been opened.)

They look out on spacious gardens, playing fields and the hutted buildings which are used for work. As the centre is on high ground there is a feeling of openness and expanse, despite the perimeter wire.

The Werrington centre, lying on a bus route to Hanley, was once an approved school. It has the small, compact, domestic look of most approved schools, but the large wire fence gives evidence of the security needs of the new institution. A small farm lies outside the perimeter and the most trusted of the inmates finish their training there—usually in parties of three and under the supervision of the farm bailiff who is part of the training staff of the establishment. Supervision is easier at this centre and the number of offences against good order and discipline is low.[20]

The Aylesbury centre is within walking distance of the town of Aylesbury. It is part of the building that was until recently a borstal institution for girls and a prison for women. Now a senior detention centre and a young prisoners' centre adjoin each other; each is enclosed by high walls and is capable of being used as a place of maximum security. The area of the detention centre is large so that, unless the staff ratio is maintained at a high level, the close supervision which the detention centre is designed to provide may not always be possible. The size of this centre also involves a great deal of maintenance, gardening and domestic work so that no outside contract work, such as making furniture, need be sought.

New centres at Medomsley, Co. Durham and New Hall Wakefield, have been established to serve the needs of the northern and north midland courts. Medomsley, once a large children's home is set high up on a hill overlooking the industrial area of Consett. It is, in winter, swept by strong winds and the atmosphere is invigorating. The grounds are large and surrounded by a high perimeter wire. A great deal of work can be done out of doors. In summer there is a swimming pool available for inmates and staff. There is a good gymnasium and a games and reading room for evening and weekend activities.

New Hall is part of the camp which is used by Wakefield prison. It is some miles from the town set in a woodland area that produces a greater impression of being enclosed and hemmed in

[20]Reports of the Commissioners of Prisons for 1958, 1959 and 1960, Tables 5c, 6c, A6.

than the other centres. A wire perimeter separates the men in the detention centre from young prisoners who are working at tree-felling outside. The buildings are extensions of the existing prison camp and they are very well fitted with showers, locker-rooms, a fine gymnasium and good kitchens.

Neither of these centres is readily accessible by any form of public transport. For this reason the staffs of the centre are restricted in their outside activities. Arrangements are made for children going to school; but transport for shopping or entertainment is not always easy so that a degree of forethought and planning is involved in every enterprise that is carried out at any distance from the centre itself. This difficulty is understood and accepted by prison staffs. It is, however, an important fact that must be taken into consideration when assessing the strain to which staffs in detention centres are subject. Yet there is some compensation for remoteness of position, in these two centres particularly. Staff clubs have been founded and the facilities of the centres themselves provide opportunities for badminton, physical training and perhaps even swimming in the summer for officers and their families. Church services in the centres are available to the staff, their families and the inmates. In this way not only has the community of prison officers and their families been drawn together, but the staff and the inmates can be unified to a far greater extent than is possible in a less remote situation.

All the centres so far described are buildings designed originally for other purposes than the penal treatment of young male offenders. The ideal design, that suggests to the inmates all that is expected of them at the centre is to be found in Aldington, Kent. It is planned as a series of one-storey buildings within a high wire perimeter. The whole centre is compact and the lay-out is such that the inmate is made to sense the pressure of the centre from the moment he enters, for it is designed to make him feel that he is passing through the admission rooms and steadily progressing through all the other units till he reaches his discharge.

The living and sleeping accommodation for the inmates varies from centre to centre. In some, as in Blantyre House or Werrington, the men sleep in long dormitories. The few cells that do exist are used for new entrants, whose habits are tested out in individual cells before they are sent into the dormitories. Security and discipline are maintained by a night-duty officer on constant patrol from end to end of the several dormitories and a low-powered light is kept on all night. Dormitories of this sort are hard to watch and it is said[21] that the number of disciplinary offences committed in dormitory establishments is higher than in centres whose accommodation is mostly in cells.

The outstanding physical characteristics of all detention centre establishments is cleanliness and order. The pattern of bright paint, highly polished floors and flowers on ledges and window sills was set in the early stages of development of the centres and it is followed in greater or less degree as new institutions are brought into use. The amount of emphasis laid on these outward signs of good order and appearance depends first on how the staff look upon the task of the detention centre. Some think that the penal or 'hard' element in the sentence of detention should be accomplished by making the standard of achievement, even in polishing floors, as near to perfection as possible. Some have other views, based perhaps on the necessity for good personal relationships between staff and inmates or upon the need for promoting good habits in the kind of work the men would return to when they left the centres. Another reason for differences in standards is simply the amount of labour available for the work that is to be done. Centres under construction need workers on outside work, on painting or on alterations and fitments indoors. Others may need little adaptation, so that the standard of domestic cleaning can be pushed as high as the staff think fit.

The regime at the centres

Each centre is subject to the Detention Centre Rules of 1952 and each follows the same general pattern of physical exercise, work and education. The men are wakened at 6.15 a.m., they change into vests and shorts, have half a beaker of hot cocoa and, in all but the hardest of weather, go to the parade ground for early morning physical training.

[21]There is, as yet, no possibility of proving this by reference to prison statistics. The remark was made by an officer of some experience, who may have been basing his judgement on observations in institutions other than detention centres. Aylesbury is the only cellular detention centre in the country.

After breakfast and inspection parade, army fashion, on the parade ground, the men are split off into sections for work. Most of this is simply cleaning and maintenance about the place, for the standard of cleanliness and order is extremely high. In each centre save Aldington, there is a mat shop or mattress shop which can be used for new entrants, or for those who need individual attention under secure conditions, or simply as a place of work when outside labour is not possible. Some centres also make wire-fencing for other government departments. There is always kitchen work to be done and this is very popular among the men, especially in the winter, so that it is often shared out to give each man no more than two weeks at this job. The report of the Prison Commissioners for 1960 shows that 162 of the effective strength of 245 in all detention centres were employed on domestic work. The salvage work of stripping telephone cables that used to be done in detention centres has stopped and in one or two centres outside contract work has been obtained. In the well-established centres there is little variety in the programme; domestic work, general maintenance and garden work occupy most of the men, most of the time. In the new centres, walls must be pulled down or built up, parade grounds made, gardens laid out, and officers' quarters painted and made ready for occupation. The men, in fact, are building themselves into their own place of detention, and, although the work is extremely hard, it is varied, constructive and purposeful. In the older centres, on the other hand, this sense of purpose in the work that is done can only be given to a few men, the most trusted and best behaved, who can work on a small farm outside the perimeter, or in the gardens surrounding it. Such assignments are very much prized. All work is supervised, although sometimes the area of supervision is large so that the men may enjoy an illusory sense of freedom.

The working day is broken by a parade after dinner and by physical training for various small groups. This involves a great deal of changing and washing. Each inmate must have a bath or a shower once a day, and a high standard of personal cleanliness and neatness is demanded. The period after tea is devoted to reading. This must be a considerable strain on those who are illiterate, but some of the more intelligent will probably enjoy the opportunity for reading something other than comics and daily papers. The selection of books is good. It is said to be much better than in prison.[22] Those who cannot read are given special lessons during the morning and good results are said to be obtained. There is, however, no scientific test of the degree of illiteracy of each offender. There may be a certain amount of lead-swinging to avoid the hard work of the morning.

Evening classes fill most of the remaining hours from tea till supper. There are all kinds of classes, English, arithmetic, science, current affairs, art, weight-lifting, motor mechanics, a referee's course for footballers and woodwork. The local education authority provides instructors and classes continue throughout the year with a short break only at Christmas and at August bank holiday. Men may select their own subject but whether there is a place for each in the class of his choice depends on the tutor-organizer's assessment of his ability and the number of vacant places in the class. In each centre there is evidence of the work done in art and woodwork classes. There are coffee-tables, stools and other hand-made wooden objects lying around in the woodwork room ready to be taken home at the end of the sentence. Drawings and paintings hang on the walls in classrooms and corridors. The standard of achievement here is unusually high[23] and reveals the great interest taken by some of the inmates in this subject. There is another aspect of the programme of evening classes which may have some importance. This is the only time during the day when the men are able to talk to, and work with, people who are not prison officers or prison officials of some sort. Some of the classes, such as current affairs, are of the kind which encourage free discussion. The men talk as much or as little as they like and it is clear that, with a good class of the more intelligent men and a sympathetic instructor, much could be done towards the formation of discussion groups which would make a positive contribution to the work of the centres.

After evening classes there is a light supper and a short period

[22]One man said in discussion that the prison libraries held a varied selection but the men were not always allowed to make their own choice. He had been given a book of plays—a translation of the plays of Aeschylus. In the detention centre he read *Gone with the Wind*.

[23]In one centre where the paintings hung up on the walls were particularly good, one of the officers remarked that the highest level of achievement in drawing and painting was reached by those who had spent some time in approved schools.

of 'association' till bed-time. For this period there are games such as draughts, chess and table tennis. The men may sit and talk or read the daily papers, of which two different papers are available each day. At week-ends a radio is available—usually tuned in to Radio Luxembourg for the latest pop-records. At week-ends too there is football in practically all weathers. In one centre the physical training instructor introduced rugby football and found it popular.

This programme of work and physical activity varies little from centre to centre, but different physical circumstances, different staff and different inmates give an individual character to each.

The staff at the centres

There is in each centre a warden, a chief officer who acts as deputy warden, a principal officer and the other members of the staff, including a medical orderly, physical training instructors, officer cooks, specialist gardeners and sometimes a woman sempstress and laundry supervisor. There is no special training for detention centre work[24] and the role of the detention centre within the penal system is interpreted to the inmates according to the character and experience of each member of the staff. In some centres each inmate is allocated to one particular officer who is responsible for his general supervision and care but it has not always been found possible to carry out this ideal of individual supervision. What happens instead is that the officer who supervises each man's daily work is the one who gets to know him best and probably sympathizes with him most. Where frequent changes of work are necessary, this personal knowledge and supervision may be lost altogether. In some cases the physical training instructor exerts the greatest influence over the men and this may be true even although he is responsible for their maximum effort. Thus, any philosophy of crime and punishment which each inmate assimilates during his stay at the centre is almost certainly derived from the observations of supervising officers as they exact

[24]Most of the members of the staff are prison officers transferred from local or regional prisons or borstals. Wardens and principal officers are given a three-day course when they are first appointed to detention centres. They are also shown around the existing centres.

from him an amount and a standard of work to which he has rarely been accustomed.

Each offender is interviewed by the warden or his deputy about five or six times during the course of a three-month sentence. He will also be brought before the warden for misbehaviour or breach of the rules; he may have contact too with the chaplain of his own denomination, who visits at least once a week; he is seen by the medical officer within twenty-four hours of his reception, and before his discharge; relatives and friends are allowed to visit several times during the course of the sentence. All these, however, are brief contacts probably seen by the inmates as being outside the context of their offence and its sentence. The major influences upon them during their ten or twenty weeks of sentence are the prison officers and their fellow-offenders.

The inmates of the centres

The men are bound together by association in the ill-luck of detection and punishment. They work together, have meals together and often sleep in dormitories where a certain amount of talking is allowed until lights out. It has been seen that those who are committed to detention centres are not generally confirmed offenders. Nevertheless each centre probably adopts the tone of the most powerful or the most numerous group of inmates. This brings about certain differences between the centres that are due to the regional differences in the offenders recruited to them.

For example, one of the new northern centres receives a high proportion of violent offenders. This is probably due to the amount of drinking and drunkenness in the area, even among young men.[25] Such men who become involved in violent acts as a result of heavy drinking are not usually criminal in the accepted sense of the term and their presence in the centre exerts a considerable influence over the whole population.

Such differences in population are reflected often in the punishments awarded to the inmates. The new centres, both in the north and in the south, are too recently established for the differences between them to have any real meaning. For the older establishments at Blantyre House and Werrington, records are available of

[25]'Offence of drunkenness,' H.M.S.O. 1960.

the offences and punishments of inmates in the course of their detention.[26]

*Table 5: Analysis of the number of disciplinary offences and the number of inmates punished in Blantyre House and Werrington Detention Centres in the years ending 31st December 1959 and 1960***

	Daily av. population	Total no. offences	Annual no. of disciplinary offences per head of daily av. population	No. of inmates punished
1959				
Blantyre House	79	274	3·5	156
Werrington	63	179	2.8	109
1960				
Blantyre House	80	173	3·4	140
Werrington	64	108	1·7	77

** Figures for 1961 show a high incidence of disciplinary offences at the new centres. There has been a sharp drop in the number of such offences at Blantyre House and Werrington.

Judging from these figures the men at Blantyre House are not so well-behaved as those at Werrington. This may be the result of a definite policy of treating every minor misconduct as an offence. In consequence, although the proportion of offences committed is high, the standards expected at the centre would seem to be high also. Nevertheless the fact that there were 224 forfeitures of remission in Blantyre House as compared with 95 at Werrington does suggest that there is a real difference in the attitudes of both inmates and staff.

The permissible forms of disciplinary punishments for reported offences are prescribed in the Detention Centre Rules of 1952. They are all based on deprivation of some sort—restriction of diet, which is very rarely imposed; reduction in seniority or grade (this involves the removal of certain small privileges); loss of earnings—an irritation rather than a real punishment since the total earned

[26]Reports of the Commissioners of Prisons for 1959, 1960, Tables 5c, A6.

is 1/6d per week; extra work, which means the restriction of leisure; removal to the detention cells for periods of sleeping, eating and leisure; confinement in detention cells; and forfeiture of remission. This last is seen by the men as the gravest punishment, and it is given more often than all the other punishments put together. Corporal punishment is not permitted by the Rules, and it is a serious offence for an officer to strike an inmate.[27]

When a man breaks the rules of the institution or is idle or insubordinate or disorderly, he is reported by the supervising officers to the warden or chief officer. His offence and its punishment is then recorded and duly appears in the annual report of the Prison Commissioners. But no institution, good or bad, could run entirely by such formal methods. More summary methods are used to keep the inmates going at the pace that the organization of the centre demands. The men talk sometimes of a 'clip round the ear-hole' being used as a swift and effective means of making them move more quickly or look less sullen. Removal to the detention cells is not always followed by an official report.[28] Where a man is removed to the cells the warden or his deputy must be told as soon as possible after the incident and permission to leave the man in the cell could then be given if necessary. Sometimes the man is left for an hour or two in the cells until he has calmed down. He may then be returned to work without a formal report being lodged. Such periods of detention in the cells do not appear in the records of punishment in the Reports of the Prison Commissioners.

There are few formal incentives to good behaviour in any detention centre. The men progress from the initial Grade I on entry to the second stage or Grade II. This grade carries certain minimum privileges such as the type of work done, and sometimes freedom to work outside the perimeter where such work is available. But the most important factor in the progress from grade to grade is that failure to reach Grade II after a certain time means loss of remission. Grade III, the top grade, is not achieved by everyone. It carries further minor privileges of

[27]See Ch. 3 p. 63. for a comment on this.

[28]Violence among the inmates may need drastic action and swift removal to detention. The Detention Centre Rules may be unrealistic when they prescribe detention in the cells only on the order of the warden or his deputy.

working without close supervision, but in the eyes of some of the men it has little value unless they appear before the court again when they believe it will count in their favour. A slight move towards more formal recognition of good behaviour has been made in the Scottish detention centre where Grade II and Grade III men wear different coloured flashes on their shoulders.

The casual incentives of friendliness from the officers, or a word of praise, cannot be recorded in the same way as punishment. That they do exist is shown by the account of the men's reaction to the officers and the behaviour of the officers to the men.

In such physical surroundings, with the rules and regimen that have been outlined, all those committed to senior detention centres serve their sentences. What this sentence is like to them and how they react to these surroundings, to the officers who are responsible for their discipline and the other inmates with whom they are confined has been reviewed by examining the attitudes of some of the young men who served their sentence in two selected centres during 1960 and 1961.

CHAPTER TWO

THE BACKGROUND AND CRIMINAL HISTORY OF THE YOUNG MEN WHO WERE THE SUBJECT OF THIS STUDY

THE principal intention of this study is to consider how the selected group of 107 young men reacted to their period in a detention centre. To do this, it is necessary to examine first their criminal records, their personal and family history and their habits at school, at work and at leisure.

The offences for which these young men were committed to the centre have been divided into five groups :

Offences of dishonesty
Offences of violence against the person
Offences of taking and driving away a motor vehicle
Other motoring offences
All other offences not included in the above four groups.

The first group covers all types of dishonesty except receiving. The offences range from the theft of a bicycle-wheel from a scrap yard or a worthless battery from an abandoned car to a carefully planned but unsuccessful robbery or a series of breakings and enterings where cars were hired to carry away the stolen goods. Included in this category are the offences of three men whose principal charge was taking and driving away a motor vehicle. They had, however, thirty to forty cases taken into consideration including many thefts from the stolen cars. These three offenders were deeply involved in dishonest activity. They changed the number plates of some of the stolen cars, picked the locks and competently adapted the stolen vehicles to their own use.

In the second group are included all offences of violence against the person, except sexual offences. The actual charges include assaults on policemen, assaults occasioning actual bodily harm or grievous bodily harm and affray. The total number of violent offenders in the sample was eighteen. Seven of them were arrested for assaulting a policeman. In four cases the police were trying to maintain law and order outside public houses and dance-halls. The degree of violence involved does not appear to have been very great and was well within the power of the police to deal with. It is natural that the accounts of these incidents given by the offenders should be favourable to themselves. Thus, for example, in several cases where a young man was charged with assaulting a policeman, he insisted that the position was quite the reverse. One man said that he was mistaken for another in a scuffle outside a dance-hall. Five cases of violence in the sample group were the result of quarrels between youths over slights or insults, whether real or imaginary. The two cases of affray were of the kind which give rise to public disquiet, since large numbers of people were involved.[1]

The third group of offences consists of cases of car-theft, either the indictable offence of stealing a motor vehicle (where the car has not been recovered within forty-eight hours) or the non-indictable offence of taking and driving away a motor vehicle without the consent of the owner. In some cases it was clear from discussion with the offenders that the taking and driving was only a preliminary to different forms of dishonest activity. In others, the young men simply borrowed a convenient vehicle, either alone or with others, and set off on a joyride. In nearly every case of this sort they had been drinking. One offender, charged with taking and driving away was proceeded against also for being drunk in charge of a mobile crane. After having a night ashore from his ship he returned to the dock area, mounted a mobile crane and drove it along the dockside.

The fourth category covers all offences of driving while disqualified.

Under the fifth heading are grouped the heterogeneous offences that remain :

[1]The two instances of race-fighting were quite separate. Each involved large numbers of young men, many of whom were probably drawn in accidentally. One of the offenders was half-coloured. He joined in the fighting on the white side.

Rape   1
Indecent exposure   3
Wilful or malicious damage   4
Having an offensive weapon or being
    a suspect person loitering in an en-
    closed place   3
Receiving   2
Non-payment of fines   5
Breach of an attendance centre order   1 [2]

It is unusual to find the charge of rape proved and the circum-stances of the offence give some clue to its criminal content. The offender is a poor specimen hanging on to the fringe of a tougher and more boisterous but younger group. They escorted a fifteen-year-old girl from a dance and committed the offence during a rough and tumble on the way home. There were four young men involved and they had all been drinking.

One of the three cases of indecent exposure presents a different problem. In the first case the charge seems to have been proved beyond doubt but the offender maintained that he was innocent, telling various stories of what happened. There was a long history of maladjusted and delinquent behaviour and three previous con-victions for indecent exposure. One psychiatric report said that punishment would have no effect on this young man. It is under-standable, however, that after four probation orders and two fines the magistrate should invoke the sanction of punishment and impose a sentence of three months in a detention centre.

The second young man had one previous conviction for indecent exposure when he was put on probation with a condition of residence in a special hostel for the deaf. He had spent the greater part of his life in institutions for the deaf and educationally sub-normal. He was, in fact, only partially deaf and, with an I.Q. of 90, far from ineducable but the combination of the two disabilities made him appear dull and unresponsive.

In the third case an eighteen-year-old offender had had three convictions for indecent exposure during the past eight months. He maintained that he could control this impulse provided he

[2]In accordance with the Criminal Justice Act, 1948, S.19, this sentence was given for the original offence which was drunk and disorderly behaviour.

had not been drinking. He had failed to make any response to probation.

The young man committed to detention after breaking an attendance centre order had received this punishment following a conviction for drunkenness and wilful damage. He had made only two attendances at the centre and had further court appearances for drunkenness.

Table 6 shows the 107 offenders grouped in accordance with the offence for which they were committed to the centres.

Table 6: The sample group analysed by offence and distinguishing between Werrington and Aylesbury

	Werrington		Aylesbury		Total	
	No.	%	No.	%	No.	%
Offences of dishonesty	21	36	24	50	45	42
Offences of violence	13	22	5	10	18	17
Offences of taking and driving away motor vehicles	8	13	10	21	18	17
Offences of driving while dis-qualified	4	7	3	6	7	6
All other offences	13	22	6	13	19	18
All Offences	59	100	48	100	107	100

The reports of the Commissioners of Prisons for 1959 and 1960 give details of the offences for which committals to senior detention centres were made. When these are arranged as far as possible in the five groups which have been described, the detention centre population for the three years 1958, 1959 and 1960 can be compared with the present sample.

It appears that the offences in the sample group as a whole are reasonably close to the proportions shown for the total 1960 detention centre population. An examination of the figures for Werrington and Aylesbury detention centres however (Table 6) shows that the Werrington sample has fewer offences of dishonesty and more of violence than the Aylesbury sample or the detention centre population as a whole.

25

Table 7: Composition of the total number of committals to senior detention centres in the three years 1958, 1959 and 1960 and the present sample of 107 offenders arranged in accordance with the offence committed and shown as percentages of the whole

	1958 %	1959 %	1960 %	Sample %
Offences of dishonesty	41	49	47	42
Offences of violence	15	17	14	17
Offences of taking and driving away motor vehicles	14	8	18	17
Offences of driving while disqualified	3	5	7	6
All other offences	27	21	14	18
All Offences	100	100	100	100

A factor in determining the offender's attitude to his penal treatment is the method by which his offence was discovered. Offences of violence are generally discovered and dealt with at once. This is true also of some offences of dishonesty where the offenders are discovered in the act of theft. For example, some inexpert youths were caught emerging from scrap yards with odd pieces of scrap and sacks of lead. A group of three reckless housebreakers were watched by a local resident as they loaded their considerable haul into a stolen car. He telephoned the police and the housebreakers were caught at once. Another group of successful thieves were caught trying to dispose of their goods to a fence. Full information on the method of detection is not always available but it is clear that roughly one in three of the dishonest offenders were given away by their accomplices, by their own families or by others who bore them a grudge.

Sometimes those who stole or borrowed cars were also given away by their friends or accomplices. More often the discovery was a complete accident—a motor-cycle stalling outside a police station, or a group of youths being asked to join in an identification parade while their stolen car lay outside. In any event several indicated that they had ample experience of car-borrowing before they were caught. For the second group of motoring offences, driving while disqualified, the pattern of detection is similar. The offences were discovered quite by accident or reported to the police by others.

Among the miscellaneous offenders there were three cases where the police took direct action and questioned the offenders on suspicion. The men were very resentful of what they thought was victimization. Two were subsequently charged with carrying offensive weapons and one with being a suspect person.

The element of chance which is present in the process of discovery and arrest is repeated in the circumstances surrounding the trial and conviction of the offender. Some courts make frequent use of remand in custody either before trial or before sentence. In others, there is no remand or bail is allowed and the offender awaits trial or sentence in his own home. Where cases are tried at the higher courts, remand in custody is much more frequent.

More than half the offenders committed to a detention centre had spent some time in prison. Offenders sent to Aylesbury, who frequently came to the centre from higher courts, were more often remanded in custody. Moreover, several of them spent long periods of from 4-8 weeks in Wormwood Scrubs, whereas few of those committed to Werrington spent more than a week in prison.

Three in every ten had the experience of trial before a superior court. For these it may be culmination of a series of events which made them well versed in all the processes of the criminal law. The criminal sophistication of the whole group however, can be demonstrated in another way—that is, by consideration of their previous offences.

Table 8 gives the previous offences of 106 offenders in the sample group. (The criminal record was absent in one case.)

Table 8: Previous offences of the sample group

	0	1	2	3	4	5+	Total
No.	17	19	22	23	12	13	106
%	16	18	21	22	11	12	100

There is no injunction to the courts in the Criminal Justice Act, 1948 concerning the committal to detention centres of offenders who had not previously been brought before the courts.

27

Table 9: *Previous offences of those committed to senior detention centres in 1959 and 1960*[3]

	0	1	2	3	4	5+	Total
1959 %	16	25	24	15	9	11	100
1960 %	14	24	23	16	10	13	100

* A change has taken place in the pattern of committals in 1961. This is discussed elsewhere.

Nevertheless, the provision in section 18 (2) that detention should only be ordered where no other method is appropriate, would seem, in all except a few cases,[4] to exclude the committal of first offenders. Every year the centres receive a considerable number of these first offenders and it would be interesting to know something about the reasons for their committal.

One-half of the seventeen first offenders in the present sample were found guilty of offences of dishonesty and several of them were involved in such offences on a large scale. Moreover, some of them admitted to an even longer history of criminality than was reflected in the number of offences dealt with by the court.[5]

There were also, however, among the seventeen, first offenders of lesser criminality whose arrival at the detention centre was surprising. It is in such cases that the exemplary nature of the detention centre sentence is most in evidence. One young man was found guilty of malicious damage. After an argument with his brother, he rushed out of the house and hurled a stone through the window of a nearby shop. He waited for the police to come and arrest him. In two separate cases of house-and shop-breaking, the offenders concerned took minor parts in these activities, for they were too dull to do otherwise. It is possible that the very dullness of their appearance contributed to the decision to sentence them to detention.

There were three offences of violence among the first offenders.

[3] Report of the Commissioners of Prisons, 1959, Appendix to Chapter 7, p. 99. Report of the Commissioners of Prisons, 1960, p. 182.

[4] Technical first offenders with many offences taken into consideration are examples of such cases.

[5] One man said that if he had been brought before the court for every offence he had committed, he would be in prison for life.

Two were sentenced for their part in a racial affray and one for an assault on his step-father, according to the offender after great provocation.

Among those who had taken and driven away vehicles there was one first offender apparently of good character and with good school and work records who, after a drinking bout became involved with some delinquent youths. Together they stole a car and, in the course of a joyride, knocked down a cyclist. Abandoning the car, they ran off leaving the injured man in the road. The offender seemed genuinely ashamed of his part in the affair but aggrieved at the severity of his sentence saying that he had had sufficient punishment in the knowledge of the injury he had inflicted.

Both in the sample group and in the total detention centre population for 1959 and 1960 the proportion of offenders who had from one to three previous offences was over 60 per cent. More than one in five, however, of all offenders sent to senior centres have a record of four and more than four offences.

The following cases illustrate the kind of offender who is sometimes committed to detention after a long history of court appearances. Two were convicted of breaking and entering and had eight and six previous offences respectively. Each had been subject to an approved school order. In the first case the court felt that the offender, after a long time in approved schools had reached a turning-point and deserved to be given the opportunity of short-term treatment. The second had an I.Q. of seventy and was considered unsuitable for borstal training. (Both were, in fact, reconvicted within three months of discharge from the centre.) A third offender has already been described.[6] He was found guilty of indecent exposure and had six previous convictions. Another young man whose I.Q. was 64 had a history of four offences and a period in an approved school for truancy. He was reconvicted within three months of discharge from the centre and was put on probation for two years.

These are examples of difficult offenders with long records of offences, but even those whose history of criminality is slight give evidence of having been involved in offences that are regarded as serious. Out of ninety cases where previous proved offences

[6]See p. 24 above.

were known to exist, seventy-six had been found guilty, at some time or another, of larceny or breaking and entering.

Various methods of treatment had been used to deal with the ninety offenders who had previous convictions. Table 10 tabulating the incidence of these measures shows that fines and probation orders were used with almost equal frequency.

Table 10: Record of previous sentences of 88 offenders found guilty of previous offences*

	Number of previous convictions				
	One	Two	Three	Four or more	Total
Fines only	6	5	4	4	19
Probation only	7	11	7	—	25
Fines and probation	1	5	9	12	27
Institutional treatment only	1	1	—	—	2
Institutional treatment or fines and/or probation	—	—	2	9	11
Other methods of disposal	4	—	—	—	4
Total	19	22	22	25	88

* Full records are absent in two cases.

Four men who had appeared before the court on more than four previous occasions had hitherto only been punished with fines or discharges. One had also been subject to a senior attendance centre order. Three out of these four had been convicted only within the past fifteen months for a series of comparatively minor offences associated with motoring, drinking or disorderliness. The fourth man, however, had a more considerable record beginning when he was fourteen years of age and including larceny and taking and driving away. The institutions to which the offenders had been committed for treatment were approved schools, remand homes and junior detention centres. There is a single instance of committal to the care of a local authority. In all cases of removal from home except one there seemed good reason for it—family indifference, inadequacy or disharmony had made institutional care seem necessary. One man had served a sentence of imprisonment for the non-payment of a fine. This was a purely coercive measure that had nothing to do with the need for treatment by removal from home. It is for consideration whether section 18 (2) a, of the Criminal Justice Act, 1948 should not have applied in this case.

There is reason to suppose that the age at which offenders are first brought before the courts has some relevance to the criminality or otherwise of their outlook and their prospects of a successful rehabilitation.[7]

Table 11 analyses this first manifestation of criminality by reference to the school leaving age, the figures are too small to make profitable any more detailed analysis.

Table 11 : Age at first court appearance analysed according to the present offence. (Total in this table is 89. Details absent in one case.)

	First finding of guilt *before* school-leaving age	First finding of guilt *after* school-leaving age
Offences of dishonesty	15	20
Offences of violence	8	7
Offences of taking and driving away	10	4
Offences of driving while disqualified	2	5
Other offences	6	12
All offences	41	48

Of those with previous court appearances 46 per cent. had appeared before the age of fifteen and there were at least seventeen boys whose first appearance was at the age of eleven and earlier, but the practice of sending to the centres those whose criminality, although serious, was only of recent origin was fol-

[7]Sheldon and Eleanor Glueck, *Later Criminal Careers*, p. 137. Mannheim & Wilkins, *Prediction Methods in Relation to Borstal Training*, Stationery Office, 1955, p. 65. Table I.

lowed in a small majority (54 per cent.) of cases. Thus more than half of all the offenders in this group have better prospects of successful rehabilitation than the others.[8]

The following account of the environment, family background and school and work record of the sample group of offenders has been collected from the records of probation officers, headmasters of schools and employers, together with the information provided in discussions with the men themselves.

The majority of the sample group comes from heavily populated and industrial areas. In Werrington the intake is mostly from Liverpool, Manchester, Sheffield and other Midland and Northern towns with a population of 75,000 or more. A few come from mining villages and one from a market town. Those committed to Aylesbury came most frequently from central or greater London. The few who do not, come from the areas of the home counties where there is known to be an overspill from London. No offender comes from a rural area. There were four men who had recently come from their home in Ireland and at Aylesbury two men came from the North, while at Werrington, one was a Londoner.

Table 12 shows the family composition of the whole group analysed by the offence which led to the sentence of detention. Following the conclusion in the Borstal Prediction Study[9] a general distinction has been made between those who lived in a family group whether it was complete or incomplete, satisfactory or unsatisfactory, and those who did not live within a family group at all.

Thus 74 per cent. of the total of 107 young men were living, at the time of the offence, in a family group of greater or less extent and cohesion. Offenders sentenced to detention for offences of dishonesty do not conform so closely to this pattern. More than one-third of them lived away from home at the time of the offence.

These figures are comparable with the borstal sample group where 73 per cent. were found to be living in households where

[8]S. & E. Glueck (loc. cit.) show that the rate of reconviction of those whose criminality is of long-standing is significantly higher than that of offenders with a recent history of crime.

[9]Mannheim & Wilkins, *Prediction Methods in Relation to Borstal Training*, p. 87.

Table 12: Table showing the composition of the groups within which the offenders lived

	Total	Living with both parents	Living with one parent and step-parent	Living with one parent	Total living in family group No.	Total living in family group %	Living with relations or or guardians	Living in lodgings	Total not living in family group No.	Total not living in family group %
Offences of dishonesty	45	20	3	6	29	64	3	13	16	36
Offences of violence	18	10	1	4	15	83	2	1	3	17
Offences of taking and driving	18	9	5	—	14	77	2	2	4	23
Offences of driving while disqualified	7	4	1	2	7	100	—	—	—	—
Other offences	19	12	2	1	15	80	2	2	4	20
	107	55	12	13	80	74	9	18	27	26

one parent at least was present.[10] There is a marked difference between both these groups of delinquent young men and a sample of male adolescents drawn from the general population where 93 per cent. lived at home.[11]

Three of the detention centre group were married. In two cases the offenders lived with the parents. In one instance the marriage had broken up and the offender returned to his family leaving his wife and two children to get on as best they could. Her maintenance allowance was regularly paid.

The size of the family group seems to show some divergence from the general pattern. Figures are available for the size of families in England and Wales. These show that 72.2 per cent. of the families in the whole country contain between one and four children. The proportion with more than four children is approximately 11.2 per cent.[12]

In the sample group the figures for family size are as follows:

One to four children in the family   63   (59 per cent.)
More than four children in the family   44   (41 per cent.)

This difference in family size between the general population and the offenders now being considered is not a phenomenon which has importance in itself. It is one more indication of the social and economic factors which press heavily upon this group. For it is a well established fact that the size of the family is generally in inverse proportion to the education, status and economic potential of the parents.[13]

Figures taken from the Registrar General's Statistical Review show that illegitimate births are approximately 5 per cent. of the total of live births. In the sample group of offenders committed to these detention centres the number of known illegitimate children was 10 or 9 per cent. In no single instance however, was an illegitimate child living apart from a natural family. In one case the child was brought up with his mother, step-father and the

[10]Ibid., p. 86, Table 25.

[11]L. T. Wilkins, *The Adolescent in Britain*, Central Office of Information, 1955, p. 8, Table 2.

[12]Carr-Saunders, *Social Conditions in England and Wales*, O.U.P., 1958, Table 3. 1. p. 25.

[13]Ibid., p. 26; W. Norwood East, *The Adolescent Criminal*, Churchill, 1942, p. 126. F. McLintock, *Attendance Centres*, Macmillan, 1960, p. 69.

children of this marriage, in complete ignorance of his true situation. In another the offender was known to be the child of a common law marriage. There is no evidence of how frequently this occurred in the rest of the group.

Although at the time of the offence 74 per cent. of the offenders were living with their families, the proportion of those who had never left home was much smaller. Only one-third of the total had lived continuously in the family group. One-sixth had spent some time in institutions, whether medical, educational or penal. Several had left home because of quarrels with their families.

The evidence of the relationship between the offenders and their families was sought from the young men themselves. The question was asked 'Do you think you get on well together as a family?' In some cases the answer was non-committal, but in at least a third of the cases where the offenders lived in a family group, they admitted the existence of tensions and difficulties beyond the normal.

One offender who said he was fairly happy at home returned each day after work to a severely depressive mother who never crossed the threshold of the house. For long periods she could not be left alone. The father protected her and waited on her, although, as the lad said, his father was not married to his mother and could have left her at any time. Another very dull-witted lad came from a problem family which suffered its latest eviction during the offender's period of detention. He had no idea where he was going on his release. The centre has since been notified that he was reconvicted within three months and has been placed on probation.

There is also an account given by one offender (and confirmed by his mother) of how he was at frequent intervals bullied, threatened and hit by his drunken father. Another young man, for far less straightforward reasons, showed a disproportionate resentment against his father, blaming him for all his misfortunes. These feelings were undoubtedly ambivalent, but the atmosphere at home must have been tense and unhappy when father and son were there together.

Several other questions were put to the offenders about their home life. 60 per cent. of the whole group declared themselves to be most fond of their mother. Only three young men admitted to a dislike of their mother. Difficulties between father or step-father and son were not readily admitted and in some cases the answer came long after the question was asked. Nevertheless, in the end, nine offenders expressed dislike of their fathers.

Discipline in the home was generally maintained by the father and correction was administered by him. Several lads described the methods of correction that were adopted. They ranged from blows with fists, sticks or belts to mere reprimands. Most of the offenders accepted the discipline that was imposed. Some hit back or argued. Many simply sulked. In some cases the mother was left to deal with her family herself. In only three instances was no attempt made to impose any discipline at all.

The cohesion or otherwise of these offenders' families was illustrated in another way. They were asked to say whether they would discuss their problems and important decisions with families, girl-friends, mates or anyone else. The answers showed that only about half of the whole group turned to their parents for advice. A rough tabulation (Table 13) of the answers shows slight difference between the Werrington and Aylesbury groups in this matter. Nearly one-third of the group kept their pressing problems from their parents, and their immediate circle of friends.

Table 13: Analysis of the answers to the question 'With whom would you discuss important decisions to do with your life?'

	Werrington	Aylesbury	Total
With parents	34	22	56
With girl-friends or mates	11	9	20
With others or with no one	14	17	31
Total	59	48	107

Only 15 per cent. of the whole sample left school either from a grammar or technical school or even the 'A' stream of a secondary modern school (Table 14). The proportion (7 per cent.) who have received any form of higher education is lower than the 14.8 per cent. given in Carr-Saunders 'Social Conditions in England and Wales' for those who received education beyond the age of fifteen.[14] The ten men who had attended residential

[14]Carr-Saunders, *Social Conditions in England and Wales*, Table 6. 44, p. 63.

schools, had been at approved schools, schools for maladjusted children, and one at a school for the dependents of naval ratings.

Table 14.

	Werrington	Aylesbury	Total	%
Grammar or Technical standard	3	5	8	7
'A' stream Secondary Modern	5	4	9	8
Secondary Modern	43	27	70	65
Residential Schools (Seconday Modern Standard)	5	5	10	9
E.S.N. Schools	2	2	4	4
Insufficient information	1	5	6	6

The records do not in all cases show how the men had progressed or behaved within the school setting but it is known that at least thirty-two (30 per cent.) had attended school irregularly; some of these were chronic truants and if the cases where there is no information are excluded from the total, this percentage would be higher. From the evidence of the Mannheim-Wilkins borstal study it appeared there was a significant relationship between a history of truancy and borstal success and failure.[15] In that study there was information concerning nearly a third of their sample of 720 men and in 28 per cent. of these cases there was evidence of truancy. One man in the detention centre sample, who had been in the 'A' stream of his secondary modern school, was reported by his headmaster to have taken an average of two days off per week throughout his school career. In twelve cases the headmaster reported that the boys were difficult, aggressive or bullying; in several cases the boy had deteriorated in his last terms at school. Only one man appeared to be wholly illiterate but several had the minimum of educational attainments.

The only clues to the intelligence of these men can be found in their levels of education, since in only ten cases were I.Q. ratings given and these appear to relate to those who are immediately recognizable as dull or had been thought to be dull. One man had

[15]Mannheim & Wilkins, op. cit., p. 97 and Table 37.

a recorded I.Q. of 64 (Wechsler), four had I.Q.'s in the low 70s, three in the low 80s and two in the low 90s. The test is not always specified. The impression gained both from the school levels and from the men's response on interview is that the majority of them fall into the low-average groups of intelligence.

Immediately on leaving school, many of these men may seem to have obtained employment of a comparatively progressive kind which could have led to skilled trades. When they were asked at the first interview whether they had any ambitions in life, they most frequently assumed that this referred to work goals, saying that they wanted to do a specific job, to do well at work, to have their own business or to earn a lot of money, but few of them seem to have made any great effort to fulfil these ambitions and employment for most of them seems to have been spasmodic, aimless and haphazard. At the detention centres, one-third admitted that they had been unemployed when they committed the offence for which they were sent there. It is true that finding work may have been very difficult in parts of the north, but this was not apparently the case in the London area, and yet only 25 per cent. of the Werrington men were unemployed at the time of their offence compared with 42 per cent. of the Londoners.[16] Several of the latter had made no efforts to obtain work. Some did casual labouring (or, in one case, golf caddying), which they found as profitable as regular work; others admitted that they lived off the proceeds of their criminal activities which brought them far more money than they could ever earn.

Three-quarters of those who were unemployed were dishonest offenders. The remainder, with the exception of two men convicted

---

[16]*Ministry of Labour Gazette*, December 1960 and March 1961. The number of unemployed males (all ages) as a percentage of the estimated total number of employees for November 1960 and February 1961 (i.e. the approximate date at which the sample were admitted to detention centre):

	November 1960	February 1961
London and South-East.	1.1	1.1
Midlands	1.4	1.8
North-West	1.9	1.7
East and West Ridings	1.1	1.0

Individual towns in the Midlands and North show percentages approximating those for London but Merseyside has the high proportion of 3.5 per cent. unemployed at both dates.

of assault, had a dishonest content to their offence. In some cases the unemployment seems to have been the cause of the offence —one or two men admit that sitting all day in cafés and coffee-bars they would be drawn into discussions of easy money making devices; others say they stole because they needed money for the lavish spending they had become accustomed to in periods of employment. In other cases the unemployment seems, in a sense, to have been the result of an offence (perhaps undetected at this point) which established that dishonesty was more lucrative than work. Few men had no history of unemployment in their work careers while some had had long and frequent periods out of work.

On the other hand among those who were employed (seventy-two), nine were apprentices or in skilled trades, and six were trainee mechanics. Apart from thirteen others who might be rated as semi-skilled or skilled workers (miners, salesmen, clerks, sheet-backers, and a chef) the remainder were chiefly engaged in un-skilled labouring or building. Some were van-drivers' or lorry-drivers' mates or were in an assortment of other jobs including window-cleaning, coal delivery, demolition, steeple jacking or factory work. Three men were in the Merchant Navy. Only one of the men who had had grammar or technical education had a commensurate job.

A rather more encouraging picture of the men's capability for work is obtained from examining how long they had stayed in their jobs. About two-thirds of the men had remained in one job for over one year and twenty-two of these had held a job for over two years (Table 15). The few men involved in offences of violence and driving while disqualified have the best records for steadiness in employment. Unfortunately, the more encouraging picture seen in this table must be qualified. Some of the men who have stayed a considerable time in one job have not necessarily been diligent or efficient workers. For example, one young man, who had been a miner since leaving school nearly five years before, had, for some time, been working only two or three days a week and had spent the rest of his time fishing and enjoying himself. Only after some time was he called before the absentee committee and disciplined. However, six men had held the same apprenticeship since they left school. As their wages in each case were appreciably lower than their unskilled contemporaries this must have required considerable strength of mind.

There is some evidence that the Werrington men had less frequently changed their jobs than the Aylesbury men. This may have been another result of the difficult employment situation in the North, whereas in the South the men could, if they wished, move more frequently back and forth from job to job. For example, one young man from the home counties had returned three times to the same timber yard after intervals spent at other jobs. Quite a number of the men had had five jobs or less since they had left school; a few had more than ten and two or three listed between thirty and forty different places of employment. A high proportion had been dismissed at least once from work for bad work or behaviour.

Table 15: The longest time spent in any one job, according to the type of their offence, by 98 men of the sample for whom there is sufficient information. The percentage of those in each offence category who have remained in one job for more than one year

	6 months or less	7 months to one year	One year or more	
			No.	%
Offences of dishonesty	6	9	27	64
Offences of violence	—	4	11	73
Offences of taking and driving away	2	5	11	61
Offences of disqualification	—	1	4	80
Other offences	1	5	12	67
All offences	9	24	65	66

Thus, the employment picture is both promising and discouraging. Generally the men are able, if they wish, to hold down a job but many are restless and impetuous in changing from job to job or lackadaisical in finding work at all. A desire for higher wages or easier money is often at the root of a man's discontent with a job.

It appears there is little difference between the alleged earnings at their last jobs of the Werrington and Aylesbury inmates. Half earned £8 per week (when in employment). A few earned over £13 but some of these were currently unemployed and must have been especially strained by the drop in income. Out of their earnings these men normally give between £2 10s and £4 for their keep to their mothers[17] or landladies. In some cases, all their wages are given and weekly pocket money returned.[18] Although a number had more than £6 to spend, the majority had between £2 – £6 for themselves.

The principal expenditure of these men, as of other adolescents,[19] is on cigarettes, drink, clothes, entertainment and on their girl-friends. Only thirteen of all the men were non-smokers. On the other hand nearly one-third smoked more than twenty cigarettes a day. This group must have found it especially difficult to adjust to the non-smoking rules of the detention centre.

Thirty men said they did not drink at all but many admit to spending more than £1 each week on drink. Some confine their drinking to one or two nights a week while others drink every night. They may drink heavily or moderately and it is often the moderate drinkers who are led into trouble by a drink too many in unusual circumstances. It has already been indicated that the offences of violence and of taking and driving away were committed frequently by men who had been drinking. In fact, for twenty-five of the present sample, drink seems to have been directly responsible for their offences. This total includes half of all the offenders using violence and half of those who had taken and driven away vehicles.

Some men spend £30 on a suit or £6 on a pair of shoes made to their own design. Haircuts and styling can be expensive and

[17]'The Youth Service in England and Wales,' Report of the Committee Appointed by the Minister of Education in November 1958, p. 23. 'The majority of the young people today appear to give their parents between £1 and £3 a week if they are living at home.'

[18]Ibid., p. 23. 'We have been told of some working-class areas of the North, centred on a few long established industries, in which the tradition that teenagers hand their wage-packet to their parents and receive pocket-money in return still largely holds.'

[19]Ibid., p. 24. '. . . those at work spend between one-sixth and one-third of their spare money on clothing and footwear . . .; another quarter is spent on drinks (soft and alcoholic), snacks, cigarettes and tobacco, sweets and chocolate; and a good part of the remainder is spent on gramophone records and record players, bicycles, motor-cycles, cinema, dancing and other entertainments, romantic magazines and paperback novelettes.'

some men are lavish with entertainment for themselves and their girl-friends. A surprising number claim some connection with a Youth Club but few are regular attenders. A small number play football for these Clubs but apart from two men who spent their time tinkering with motor bicycles and doing repairs for friends and another who went camping at weekends with a friend, none of the others mentioned any interesting hobbies or leisure-time pursuits. Their entertainment is chiefly found in dance-halls, cinemas, jive clubs, coffee-bars, billiard halls and, for the London men, occasionally in West End clubs. Many of the men have motor-cycles. Some have cars which they buy and sell with great rapidity. Sometimes a group of friends will hire a car at the week-end and invade a neighbouring town for fresh entertainment. One inmate received a letter from a friend at home describing how the local youths had started hiring new cars at £4 per day at the week-ends and using them to take as many of them as possible on drinking excursions to Blackpool and other neighbouring towns. Rarely did a man on interview say that he spent an evening at home, unless it were playing records or watching television with a girl-friend at his or her home.

When these young men start courting they tend to spend their time exclusively with their girl-friends although several said they were allowed one or two evenings off each week to go out with their mates. Sometimes this was the occasion of their getting into trouble. Table 16 below shows that nine of the men said they went around exclusively with girl-friends. Several of the more deprived and rootless young men had become deeply attached to a fiancée or girl-friend. It is not surprising that both for them and for

Table 16 : *Companionship of the total detention centre sample*

	With girl-friend only	Alone	With one or two friends	Gang or group of three or more
No.	9	12	41	45
%	9	11	38	42

others a breach or quarrel with a girl-friend is very unsettling. For example, one young man, because he had quarrelled with the fiancée he had known for two years, said that he deliberately spent several evenings getting drunk to forget. As a result he had committed the assault for which he was at the centre.

Half of the men said that they had girl-friends whom they had known for varying lengths of time but most of them had other friends with whom they spent their leisure.

Few of the men admit to solitary habits and those who do, on the whole, form an unhappy group of inadequate or maladjusted men. An almost equal number of the others associate with one or two special friends or mix with a group of three or more. Only five of the latter (and one more who, although essentially a lone-wolf, occasionally aligned himself with a gang) admitted to being members of gangs in the strict sense. Several of the others belonged to more loosely-knit groups of six or more, meeting casually, or by arrangement, in a café, coffee bar, or public house. In London the meeting place was sometimes a dance-hall. Some of these gang or group members found themselves in their present predicaments as a result of this allegiance, for example, the two men involved in affrays and another immature youth who said he broke and entered because his gang would have sneered at his lack of courage if he had not done so. Table 17 shows that more offenders involved in violence and in taking and driving away associate in groups or gangs than is customary for the sample as a whole. The dishonest men are a little less gregarious. On the other hand, Table 18 demonstrates that not many of these dishonest offenders actually commit their offences alone. Of those who did act alone, two took money from meters at their homes, others stole from shop-counters or houses and one man took the contents of his land-lady's handbag from her bedside. Over half the dishonest offenders committed their offences with one or two accomplices whereas comparatively few set off in a group. For the others, the type of offence determined whether there were associates or not. For example, with the take and drive away offenders, where the offender has taken a vehicle for a ride simply because he 'likes cars' he will probably be alone; where there is a more deliberate intention to joy-ride or to use the vehicle for other activities he may have as many companions as will fit into the car to aid and abet the enterprise.

From the accounts that the men gave of their current offences, it was clear that many of them had deliberately planned their dishonest activities. It is difficult, however, to discern at what point an offence becomes planned. This must be particularly so where a group of men meet casually and then, as they often put it, 'decide to do something'. It is also difficult to differentiate between the intentions of friends who meet to commit the offences and those who commit the offence because they have met and are

Table 17: Offences committed by men who normally associate with a group or gang of friends and by those who have fewer associates

Associates with:	Offences					
	Dis-honesty	Violence	Taking and driving away	Driving while dis-qualified	Others	All
Group or gang	17	10	11	0	7	45
Alone or 1–2 friends only	28	8	7	7	12	62
All	45	18	18	7	19	107

Table 18: Companions of offenders in the commission of the offence for which they were sent to detention related to the type of that offence

	Alone	With 1–2 others	With a group or gang
Offences of dishonesty	7	25	13
Offences of violence	7	5	6
Offences of taking and driving away	8	5	5
Offences of driving while disqualified	6	1	—
Other offences	14	3	2
All offences	42	39	26

at a loss for something else to do. In some cases, there was no doubt that there was thoughtful planning and some organization, as for example, in the planned robbery or the large scale car-borrowing. In others, there is no doubt that the offence was entirely unpremeditated and impulsive. As one man said, 'I have never stolen

anything unless it was just lying around waiting to be taken.' However, in twenty-seven out of the forty-five cases of dishonesty (60
per cent.) it can be said that there was at least some degree of calculation in the offence. In each of these cases the man was with at
least one other. Moreover, where the dishonesty was committed by
a group of men, it was always planned, with two exceptions where
the group of men had come out of a public house and committed
the offence in a fit of bravado. On the other hand, only three
of the offenders who took and drove away could be said to have
planned their offence and all these were jointly charged. Only one
man deliberately assaulted a contemporary after lying in wait for
him.

Table 19. Age on admission of offenders

	Years of age				
	17	18	19	20	Total
Offences of dishonesty	18	16	9	2	45
Offences of violence	6	5	4	3	18
Offences of taking and driving away	11	4	2	1	18
Offences of driving while disqualified	—	3	1	3	7
Other offences	5	6	3	5	19
All offences	40	34	19	14	107

Table 19 shows that the men were all, as prescribed by the
Criminal Justice Act, 1948, between seventeen and twenty-one
years of age. These figures show a preponderance of younger
offenders in the sample group. 70 per cent. of the total are seventeen and eighteen years of age. Offenders who have taken and
driven away vehicles tend to be younger, as a group, than the other
offenders whereas the violent offenders are older. There were, indeed, noticeable differences in the maturity of offenders of different
ages, from the two youths who had only attained seventeen years
while awaiting trial and sentence (one of whom had been sent
in error to a junior centre before being transferred to his senior
centre) to a few, more adult, sometimes more sophisticated nineteen and twenty-year olds. Details are not available of the ages
of offenders committed to all detention centres during 1960, but

the Prison Commission have kindly supplied figures to show the age-structure of the group committed to detention centres in 1961. In this year, at least, the offenders committed to senior centres were younger than those, within the same age limits, who were committed to prison. In the matter of age they resemble the borstal committals of which 66 per cent. were aged eighteen and under.

Although they may have differed considerably in their maturity and their physical appearance, there were, among the sample only two men with real physical disabilities. One had a history of asthma for which he received remedial exercises at the centre and another was handicapped by deafness. In general the men were of good physique but six had records of treatment in mental hospitals or schools for maladjusted children. A seventh had refused mental treatment, although it was thought necessary in his case.

All the men were subject to the same regime at the centre. Their sentences differed in only one respect. Whereas the majority had been committed to the two centres for three months' detention, a smaller number was subjected to longer sentences or shorter orders resulting from the non-payment of fines. The following table (Table 20) shows that by chance, more men in the sample

Table 20: Length of detention centre order of the 107 men of the sample at Werrington and Aylesbury detention centres compared with the orders of the detention centre population as a whole in 1960

Length of Order	Werrington	Aylesbury	Both		Total Detention Centre Committals for 1960	
	No.	No.	No.	%	No.	%
Two months and under	5	1	6	6	21	3
Three months	48	33	81	76	569	86
Four months	—	6	6	6	26	4
Five months	—	—	—	—	3	—
Six months	6	8	14	13	46	7

were subjected to these less usual orders than was the case for the detention centre population as a whole in 1960. Of those who were committed for the non-payment of fines, two completed two-months, one one-month and two 'bought' their discharges in less than a week. The remaining man, among those with short orders, served one month. Having failed to comply with the attendance centre order he was brought before the court and was committed for his original offence of drunkenness. All these men, knowing they had only a short term to complete or that they might be able to pay their fines and gain their discharge, could approach their period of training more light-heartedly than those who were embarking on longer terms. However, at this early stage those with four or six-months' sentence did not appear, on this account, to be more resentful, than the others. In several cases they seemed to count themselves lucky to have avoided an indeterminate borstal sentence.

A further analysis of the few four and six-month sentences shows that all except one of those awarded to the Werrington men in the sample were awarded by magistrates' courts while over half of the Aylesbury men with longer orders were committed by superior courts. There was one successful appeal among the Aylesbury men against a four-months' order and one six-months' order had been reduced to four months. Table 21 gives brief details of some of the circumstances leading to these longer sentences.

Whatever the length of the order, however, the programme of the training was the same and it does not seem that the unequal time they expect to serve unduly affected the attitudes of the men when they were admitted to the detention centres and were initiated into the regime.

Table 21.

Offenders	Length of sentence	Sentencing Court	Offence	Circumstances
Werrington				
2	6 mths.	Mag.	Meter-breaking	Living in house occupied by reputed criminals.
1	6 mths.	Assizes	Affray	Racial fight between two groups. First offender.
1	6 mths.	Mag.	Larceny	The theft followed a drunken fight with coloured men. The offender had failed to answer bail and returned to Ireland.
1	6 mths.	Mag.	Larceny	With one other picked up scrap. Had previous junior detention centre order.
1	6 mths.	Mag.	Take and drive away	Only one previous offence but ex-Approved school (truant).
Aylesbury				
1	6 mths.	Mag.	Meter-breaking	Appeal upheld.
1	6 mths.	Mag.	Grevious bodily harm	Beat up the master in charge of a group of youths who remarked on his hair style.
2	6 mths.	Sessions	Breaking and entering and larceny	A number of cases on an organized basis. One—first offender.

Table 21:—cont.

Offenders	Length of sentence	Sentencing Court	Offence	Circumstances
Aylesbury				
2	6 mths.	Sessions	Breaking and entering and larceny	Unsuccessful attempt but large amount of property involved. Both first offenders but a co-offender had considerable record.
1	6 mths.	Sessions	Receiving stolen car	Intelligent, self-satisfied young man with previous offences.
1	6 mths.	Old Bailey	Actual bodily harm	Originally charged with robbery with violence, then reduced to G.B.H. and A.B.H. Co-offender to borstal. One previous offence.
3	4 mths.	Mag.	Take and drive away and larceny	A large No. of offences taken into consideration; highly organized.
1	4 mths.	Appeals	Take and drive	Reduced from Magistrates' court's 6-month sentence. 4 previous offences (2 minor).
1	4 mths.	Old Bailey	Actual bodily harm	Gang-fight between two groups of young men. Originally G.B.H.
1	4 mths.	Old Bailey	Conspiracy to rob	Kept watch for mate who made an unsuccessful wages-snatch at small factory where he worked.

CHAPTER THREE

THE FIRST INTERVIEW

IN accordance with the research plan, each of the men in the sample was interviewed within two to eight days of his arrival at one of the two detention centres. The first questions of this initial interview have provided some of the background material contained in the previous chapter and were designed to place the man in his home setting and to discover some of his attitudes to life in the community. Later questions in this first interview were concerned with the man's attitudes and reactions to his sentence and the first stage of his training.

By the time that they were interviewed, the men had, in many cases, changed from smartly-dressed and long-haired or ill-kempt and sloppy youths into close-cropped and uniformly dressed young men. However they might disguise it, they were uncertain and shocked by the sequence of events which led to their admission to the detention centre. Some were outraged; others were frightened, nervous, resentful. Some were outwardly tough and arrogant; others were despairing and tearful. Very rarely did it seem that a man was untouched by the impact of his arrival at the centre. Such is this impact, that later the men feel convinced that there is a deliberate policy to make the first hours and days unforgettably unpleasant and that the officers chosen for their reception are especially selected for their harshness.

Previous knowledge of detention centre treatment

Even the most sophisticated of these young men cannot fail to be apprehensive when he is sentenced and when he arrives at the gates of the centre, despite the fact that more than half of the sample said that they had heard of detention centres before their own committal to them. Seven in every ten of the Aylesbury sample claimed to have heard about detention whereas only half as many at Werrington had. There may be two main reasons for this difference between the men at the two centres; reasons which could also add to or detract from the man's initial awe of detention. In the first instance, the Aylesbury men tend to come from a comparatively limited area. Often they have friends among past or present inmates of the centre or have frequented the same clubs and dance-halls as others. They often come with others from Sessions courts or through Wormwood Scrubs. The Werrington men, on the other hand, come from a widely scattered area. It is true that the Liverpool and Manchester men tend to come from certain streets and neighbourhoods of their cities and through Crown courts, but many men were committed from smaller magistrates' courts. The second reason may be that more Aylesbury men than Werrington men have spent some time in prison.[1]

At both centres the majority of men who had any knowledge of detention said that their informants were friends or acquaintances, but a number said that they had heard of it whilst in prison. In fact a far greater proportion of those who had been in prison, for any length of time, than of those who had not, knew of detention as an existing form of punishment. At the same time, those detained or remanded in prison were probably also the more criminally sophisticated: a consideration which is, perhaps, confirmed by the fact that also proportionately more dishonest offenders in the sample knew of detention. Four of the sample had already been in junior centres and should have known what to expect; three men said their information came from the newspapers, but it seems that they had read little more than the accounts of the cases in which some young men were sent to detention centres.

In most cases, what the young men had heard of detention centres was vague. In some they had simply heard of their existence. At the date at which the Aylesbury men were seen they would have heard details of Goudhurst or a junior centre only. Their first impressions seemed to be that the regime at the new Aylesbury centre was not as hard as they had been led to expect by their informants. The Werrington men would have had infor-

[1]See Chapter II, p. 27.

mation about Werrington itself or the other junior centre. The majority of the men at both centres said they had heard that detention centres were 'very hard'. Among the details that they had heard were some destined to make them apprehensive—'everything is on the double', 'you dig holes and fill them in', 'you scrub all the time', 'they beat you up' or 'the food is bad'. However, several had more comforting informants who told them that it was 'not bad', 'the food is good', 'it makes you fit', 'it is only like the Army', and that a junior centre had been 'like a holiday camp'.

Attitudes of the sample to alternative forms of treatment

How then, do these men regard their sentence and how do they compare their punishment with other forms of treatment they might have received? Would they have preferred one of the alternative sentences that were, in some cases, allotted to those accused with them? According to the offenders themselves, about half of them had offended in company. Some men alleged that their accomplices had either not been caught or not been charged. Forty-five of the sample knew that their co-offenders had been dealt with by the courts and that the most severe sentence that any one of their companions had received was as follows:

Borstal	12
Prison	7
Detention Centre	15
Probation Order	7
Fine	4

(For this purpose, borstal is adjudged as 'more severe' than prison, in view of the men's dislike of the length of sentence.) Thus, thirty-four of these men had co-offenders who received either more severe or equal treatment. In this respect, only the few (11) whose co-accused had been more leniently treated could feel resentful.

Prison

Sixty-four of the men had spent some time in prison.[2] For a few this was only a day or two but over half of them (regardless of the

[2]All save one had been awaiting trial or sentence; the length of time spent is discussed in Chapter II.

length of time spent) said they found this experience better than their first few days at the detention centre. The chief reason given was that life was easier in prison where they were allowed to lie in a cell most of the day and that no one 'bothered' them. Other advantages were better food (particularly for men at one centre), being allowed to smoke and having more visitors. One may have verbalized another more general feeling that 'you are treated like men in prison'. However, the men did not necessarily prefer their idea of prison even if they thought some aspects preferable. There are, for instance, divergent attitudes to the quicker tempo of the detention centre which helped pass the time more quickly and left no time for boredom. Several found the cleanliness and physical conditions of the centres preferable. Some did not feel the same sensation of being locked in at the detention centre (especially at Werrington) as they had experienced in prison where they were often locked in their cells during the day. Two men actually claimed to prefer the discipline and strictness of detention—one because it would do him good, the other because he would have no opportunity for contamination by older offenders. One man may have expressed the attitude of the more blasé when he concluded that prison was pointless.

Borstal

A man's attitudes to his treatment are certainly influenced by boredom and deprivation of privileges but, above all, they are influenced by the length of sentence and for this reason all but eight men said they thought they would prefer their detention centre treatment to borstal training.[3] Knowledge of it was varied but probably more widespread than knowledge of detention at this date. The general impression was that borstal would be easier, particularly because they thought that you normally go to an open borstal first. There would be more privileges—television, pictures, entertainment, better food and, above all, smoking. A few said they would have been able to learn a trade at borstal. Other advantages that they saw in borstal were that 'you are not

[3]None of the men had, of course, undergone borstal training, but no one denied having heard of it. Several had friends or relations who had experienced it.

53

pushed around' and that the atmosphere would be conducive to better relations with the officers.

Reasons related to length of sentence, which some men gave for their preference for detention centre training over borstal were that they might brood in the more leisurely atmosphere, or that they might be affected by the more serious offenders and compare notes in their spare time. By 'cramming everything into a short time you realize more quickly'.

The eight men who thought that borstal might have been better or preferable for them, despite the length, included two ex-approved school boys who were so inured to all forms of treatment that the length did not weigh heavily with them. One wanted to be anywhere other than where he was at that moment; the other, a border-line defective (who might have been sent to borstal for his current offence if he had not been considered too dull to profit from the training) wanted to join a friend there. Three other men had home circumstances which were such that a long period away would be a comparatively acceptable prospect. Another three seemed to think borstal might provide an easier alternative with more privileges and less effort demanded.

Probation

Many of the men think they should have been awarded the non-institutional alternative of probation. Two-thirds of them had been on probation at least once in their lives and nearly a quarter had had two or more experiences of it. More of the Werrington men had already had these two chances but at both centres many had also already been placed on probation since they were 'adult' (i.e. seventeen years). In the majority of cases the probation officer provided a report for the court and this report was with the man's records at the centres. In a number of these reports the probation officer had recommended detention; in others, he had said that further supervision would be of no value. One probation officer wrote to the Warden :

'. . . it is a good thing that he was found guilty as he recently got away with an assault case. He might well have graduated to more serious crime . . . he seems a good detention centre case, . . . he is likely to try to swing the lead, I should think, and it will be useful for him to find he cannot do so. He is bright enough to profit

54

by a sharp lesson but if he can make it an easy time, his respect for all forms of authority will be dangerously lessened. In a way he needs the punitive element in his detention, because if he can learn that this (deterrent punishment) does happen, can be accepted and got over with no loss of face, this will do more for him than the relatively easy option of supervision alone.' In such cases as this, where detention was recommended to the courts, and in others where the probation officer did not oppose it, the men were usually resentful and aggrieved. At this point in their careers less than half of the sample thought that there was any value in probation as a form of treatment for themselves. This is not very surprising as so many of them had just failed as probationers. One or two admitted that it might have been useful if they had 'bothered' to report. Several found reporting an irritation—'you have to queue after work', 'it got on your nerves', 'it is no punishment', 'it's just talking', 'he always said the same thing' and 'they can't tell you what to do, can they?'. One or two rather inadequate youths complained that their probation officers had failed to find them accommodation to their liking and one man said that his officer tactlessly arrived always at teatime, just as the family returned from work. These complaints were exceptions however for, in general, the men seemed at least to respect their probation officers, even though they might regard probation as valueless.

Attitude to sentence of detention

Two-thirds of the men answered a question 'why do you think that the court thought it was necessary for you to be sent away from home this time rather than to allow you (further) supervision at home?'. The majority of those who answered had previous offences and previous experience of probation. They, therefore, presumed that they were 'sent down' because of their records, because they 'did not learn', because other treatment had been ineffectual or they had committed a breach of an order. In three cases they thought they had been sent away as an example to others, two (probably justifiably) said that it was because of the seriousness of their offences, three because of their bad associations or alleged gang membership, and one because of the judge's alleged policy, and one simply because he thought the court was sorry for the step-father he had assaulted and injured.

These offenders undoubtedly consider they have rights in relation to punishment. They have their own tariff system which graduates through fines and probation to detention, borstal and prison, probably in that order, but, despite the fact that two-thirds of them had already been given a chance on probation and more had been fined and that they have already dismissed probation as valueless, there was still an implication in many of their answers that they should never have been sent away at all. This illogicality is typical of the lack of consistency that was often found in individual men's answers to successive questions. Furthermore, they were asked in another question whether they considered that detention was the right punishment for them. Half of the men in the sample claimed that it was not, principally because they did not think they deserved to be sent away at all. In a few cases only did they repudiate the sentence because they deserved any more severe treatment and there were a few others by whom it was rejected because they either denied the present offence or the gravity of it. However, nearly half of the Aylesbury sample[4] and half of all the dishonest offenders admitted that detention was probably the right treatment for them. On the other hand, less than one-third of the Werrington men, and of the offenders other than dishonest ones, accepted the sentence as 'right for them'.

From the answers which the men gave to this question whether detention was the right punishment for them, it appeared that they interpreted 'right' as meaning either deserved or suitable in either a punitive or reformative way. Some allowed their personal preferences to colour their answers. All the Werrington first offenders felt that they should have been put on probation or fined on this occasion; half the Aylesbury first offenders felt the same or at least expected such treatment. One of the Aylesbury men thought he deserved borstal; one thought six months too long although he admitted detention was 'right' for him; a third first offender accepted his sentence as 'deserved' but questioned its value for himself.

Since so many of them protested that detention was not the

[4]Some of the differences in the proportions of the answers given by the men at the two centres are influenced by the proportion of Werrington men (10 per cent.) who gave a non-committal or 'don't know' answer to this question. 8 per cent. of the offenders with other than dishonest offences were similarly non-committal. All the Aylesbury men gave some answer.

right punishment for themselves or for their offences and some thought that they deserved less severe punishment, an attempt was made to discern the type of man for whom they considered the centres were suitable. After their first few days at the centres, their ideas of the suitable detention centre inmate fell into the following broad categories :

Violent types (tough, aggressive, 'big-heads', bullies etc.)	27
Dishonest offenders	3
Repeated offenders ('don't learn')	10
First offenders	10
Lazy, work-shy, (wasters, loafers, street-corner boys)	7
Anyone, others like himself	12
No one and not himself	15
Other types (named friends, relations etc.)	9
No answer, not understood.	15

Just as the general public have grown to regard detention centres as places for hooligans and thugs, the largest number in the sample thought that the centres were most suitable for these 'tough' boys who think themselves 'big'. A quarter of the men giving this description had themselves been involved in offences of violence. None of the three who thought the centres suitable for dishonest offenders had committed such offences themselves. It is surprising that the same number of men thought it suitable for first offenders as thought it right for more frequent offenders. The young men who thought it was the right place for poor workers had all themselves average work records. Four Werrington men thought the centre would be good for specified, and usually disliked, friends or relations : three Aylesbury men suggested it was only suitable for the 'less rough' types from good and respectable homes, one man thought it suitable only for younger boys and one strictly for the very athletic. Some did think it was suitable for themselves and anyone like them but, on the whole, it seems that if they think detention at all suitable for anyone it is someone other than themselves. Fifteen at this stage pronounce it suitable for no one.

In many cases, therefore, they do not consider detention suitable for themselves nor do they think it suitable for the type of offences that they have committed.

In describing the circumstances of the offences for which they were sent to the detention centre very few men expressed any remorse or showed any shame. While there were only three men who admitted that they did not mind robbing or thieving for 'laughs', equally few admitted that they had committed a serious offence. Some of the more seriously involved dishonest offenders made no effort to minimize their criminality but it was usually left to the less implicated first offenders to be regretful. Several men admitted to leading dishonest or delinquent lives before being caught on their current offence and were prepared to accept their sentence for their previous records rather than for their present offence. Most of the accounts were more concerned with the way in which the offenders had been detected and it was this that they usually regretted and resented most. Among the young men who had taken and driven vehicles, several said that they were returning the vehicles when caught and felt that this should have exonerated them. They showed little sympathy for the car-owners whom they knew to be covered by insurance. Certainly few of those sentenced for car offences felt they had committed acts which deserved such treatment and all inmates appeared to support this view. The resentments of some of the men who had committed assaults have already been mentioned, but it appears that, with the exception of 'fair fights' between contemporaries, the majority of men (including those convicted of violence themselves) do disapprove of assaults of any kind and particularly did they pro-scribe grievous bodily harm. Several appeared to consider that youth and a search for 'kicks' or 'giggles' excused almost any offence; others regarded drink, unemployment, family disputes, provocation or the comparative wealth of their victims as absolv-ing factors.

The whole question of their attitudes to certain offences was taken one stage further when the men were asked whether there were any offences they would hesitate to commit. Their answers are similar to those that the Wardens said that they obtained—most of the men said they would only refrain from murder or rape. Many of them censured sexual offences, especially with young girls and boys, and violence to old ladies and children. Twenty-two men in the sample said they would not rob and the same number said they would not commit dishonest acts where the old, the infirm, their mates or working-class homes were involved. A quarter of the men, blaming either special circumstances or an isolated lapse (drink, impulse, opportunity, bad company or a passion for cars) for their current offences, said they would not commit any offence. Three men implied that the risk of getting caught would deter them; for example, one said he would not rob a bank because he did not have the brains. Several said inadequately, but realistically for them, that they did not know as 'you can't tell until you have done it'. Only a few men were very anxious to establish that they were not to be identified with delinquents.

Early attitudes and reactions to the detention centre regime

It has been seen that among the things that the men most dislike about any treatment is the loss of privileges—smoking, drinking, entertainment and a good time; but inherent in all institutional treatments is the loss of freedom and removal from home. Thirty-seven have never been away from home before but, on the other hand, by the time they reach the centre, two-thirds of the sample have had some time, however short, in prison. Three men had been in the Army, five in the Merchant Navy, four in junior detention centres and eighteen in approved schools, children's homes or residential schools which implies that these had already experienced establishments with regimes which were in some ways similar to detention, either being disciplined or, at least, in occasioning enforced removal from home.[5] Many more had been, by choice, away from home.

The loss of the companionship and support of their friends and girl-friends may undermine their self-assurance. Sixteen men in the sample were fortunate in this respect as they were admitted to the centre with a co-offender who was usually also a friend. The majority of men with girl-friends at home thought that the girls would remain faithful to them while they were away. The majority of these expected to receive letters from them. The few men who had recently been rejected by girl-friends either as a result of their court appearance or for other reasons were unhappy and depressed.

To summarize the men's attitudes to alternative or actual sentences, it seems that all the men would unmistakably have

[5]Even as those who had been away from home before were at some advantage at the centres, so also were the thirteen who did not smoke and the twenty-two who said they did not drink.

preferred not to receive a sentence involving loss of liberty but, if institutional treatment was inevitable, then the majority preferred the prospect of detention to the alternatives. A few see advantages in a short-term of imprisonment and some are resentful because they pleaded not guilty or mitigating circumstances. The mood in which they arrived at the centre was determined by this acceptance or rejection of conviction and sentence and would predispose them to accept or reject the actual training programme.

Two-thirds of the men confessed to feeling very miserable and homesick during the first days of their detention but half of these had already settled more happily by the time that they were interviewed. Of the remainder, a few (15) said they were fairly happy, unconcerned or 'not bothered'; some (19) simply said they were bored or 'fed-up' because of what they were missing outside. Nearly all the men who had never been away from home before had been, at least initially, very unhappy, although a few had settled within the first two or three days. Those who settled quickly tended to be the duller youths or those who had difficult home relationships or who had already experienced living away from home.

Among the questions that the officers were asked on their questionnaire (which will be discussed below) was one concerning the men's initial adjustment to the centre. The officers' assessments[6] could be roughly divided into three categories—miserable, bewildered, anxious (57); settled easily, happy-go-lucky (5); surly, aggressive, resentful, swaggering (38).

It seems that the officers agreed that the men were miserable and homesick in the majority of cases but half of the few men (38) who were said by the officers to have been initially surly and difficult were according to their own reckoning, unhappy at first. The only man who settled easily and was seen by the officers to have done so was a very dull youth. On the whole, therefore, there seems to have been little effort on the part of the men to disguise their feelings from the officers. Some, however, apparently did try to hide their true feelings for, among a handful of men who

[6]At Werrington, where four separate officers reported on each man, the assessments of one of the two house officers who had reported on most of the men are used here. At Aylesbury, there is only one house officer's report on each man.

were in or near to tears when they were interviewed, one was described by the reporting officers as being 'cheeky' initially. He was completely overcome in the interview by any mention of home and eventually begged that it should not be mentioned. Another man (like the former, at the centre for an offence of violence) also burst into tears at the interview and was very discomfited when an officer entered the room. He too had been reported by the officers as 'swaggering' and as having settled down quickly.

On the whole, on interview, the men were not as resentful of their arrival at the centre as some of their responses to questions indicated. One disturbed but intelligent man was very distressed (and subsequently absconded) because he claimed that he had been sent for treatment similar to that which he had received throughout his life from an unsympathetic father whom he blamed for his adverse circumstances. He was therefore unable at this point to accept any part of the disciplinary regime.[7] Two other young men who were excessively resentful had, it appeared, arrived with flowing and elaborate hair styles which had been cut. This they were not able easily to forget. One of these young men, again a very unstable man who had had a period in a mental hospital following an attempt at suicide and who was rejected by his home, was too bitter to be prepared to answer many of the questions. Another man said that he had had people shouting at him all his life so that the detention centre represented nothing new but that he needed something different to 'cure his inferiority complex'. Differences in maturity were also evident in the attitudes displayed at interview. The 'little boys' were unsure of themselves, bewildered, protesting, panicky or adopting a cheeky bravado. The older men, or those who wished to impress with their comparative maturity, were more often confident, resentful, disdainful or superior.

As a result of the events in the first few days at the detention centre, many of the men were more than ready to talk of their experiences and of their feelings about the individual components of their training. Some were monosyllabic; some found it difficult to understand any of the questions; others may not have under-

[7]His adjustment was not improved by the fact that he alleged that the prison psychologist had said that detention centre training would not be suitable for him as it represented the type of discipline from which he had been trying to escape all his life.

stood fully. Without a doubt, almost all of them were cautious in their answers to the more committing questions that followed and they may have either exaggerated or under-stated their real feelings or have given an answer which they thought would please. Their mistaken interpretation of the role of the interviewers was illustrated, at one centre, by the fact that they thought that if enough of them complained about the food something would be done about it. Even within these limits, however, and despite other difficulties of communication, some insight was gained into the men's underlying attitudes and reactions to the activities in which they participated and to the people they encountered at the centres.

By the time that they were interviewed the men had had their first experience of all aspects of their training. They had had their first taste of circuit training, of early morning rising and physical training, of drill and marching, of meal time routines, kit lay-outs and parades, of saying 'yes sir, no sir', of jumping to attention, of changing ten to twelve times per day, of scrubbing, of their daily hour of association and recreation.[8] There emerge from their experience of these few days eleven major sources of irritation or grievance. Each of the men were asked three allied questions :

A. What do you dislike most about the detention centre?
B. Is there anything which you think should be changed?
C. What do you chiefly hear the older inmates complaining about?
D. Describe the daily programme at the centre and say what you think about the various activities.

In answering the first question the men were probably stating simply their own immediate and most deeply felt source of vexation and wretchedness, which they identified with the purely retributive and deterrent element of the training. The second question allowed them to make suggestions for removing these vexatious elements and substituting more tolerable factors or, even, more reformative and constructive activities. The answers to the third question may have represented either the man's own unexpressed complaints attributed to others, or a general, conversational 'grumble'. In a few cases the answers to all three questions were the

[8]They had not usually experienced evening classes; and they had not always played football. Most of them had seen the Warden or Chief Officer.

same but most men gave different answers of differing intensity to each. Table 22 gives the distribution of the answers to the three questions A, B, and C. Table 23 shows the number of men who, in reply to question A, B, or D, made either an adverse or favourable comment on any of the aspects of their training.

At both centres the men chiefly resented and suffered from the lack of cigarettes and, in fact, the figure shown here is considerably lower than the true one as the men were always asked to give an alternative answer if they readily could. The same is true for the Aylesbury men in relation to the quantity of food[9] but they complained that their hunger was aggravated by the lack of cigarettes and vice versa and their obsession with these two restrictions overshadowed all other grievances. The Werrington mens' food grievances were usually of the conventional type concerned with quality and personal dislikes. For both centres, getting up early and doing physical training was one of the major sources of grievance. This was more understandable at Werrington where the men were interviewed in the winter when there was snow, ice, rain and cold winds, but even at the more temperate Aylesbury it appears to have been disagreeable for a number of men.

But both tables (within the limits of the small numbers) indicate a clear difference between the reactions of the men at the two centres. At Werrington, many of the men disliked specific parts of the programme. They appeared less able to 'take' the physical exertions, the strict discipline, the way they considered the officers treated them and the penal atmosphere (i.e. being locked up and being ordered around). Over a third of them objected to physical training or circuit training at this early stage, making comments such as—'it is cruelsome for those not used to it', 'it sends you daft', 'it is impossible for the weak' and 'it is too much for my offences'. Drill, marching and parades also went against the grain for a number of them, although these were not often their major aversions. Several of them found drill difficult; one very dull youth realized that he was 'an idiot' at it; another complained about drill because he alleged that he had been "punched for mucking-up a parade'. The greater vulnerability of these Werrington men may have been partly due to the factors previously mentioned, that

[9]It was acknowledged officially that, due to early administrative, difficulties, food was only just adequate at this stage. By the second interview complaints about the quantity of food were retrospective only.

Table 22: Analysis of answers to questions A, B and C above by the Werrington and Aylesbury men

	Werrington			Aylesbury			Both		
	Dislike A	Would change B	Others' complaints C	Dislike A	Would change B	Others' complaints C	Dislike A	Would change B	Others' complaints C
1. No smoking	5	6	8	10	4	10	15	10	18
2. Food	2	2	10	9	4	37	11	6	47
3. Early rising and early P.T.	10	7	4	4	10	1	14	17	5
4. Officers and their alleged treatment	10	4	15	4	3	2	14	7	17
5. P.T. and circuit training	8	6	7	—	2	1	8	8	8
6. Strictness, discipline and respect	7	—	2	2	—	—	9	—	2
7. Marching, drill, and parades	3	3	1	1	2	—	4	5	1
8. Tempo, 'rushing'	6	—	1	1	3	1	7	3	2
9. Changing	3	4	2	4	8	6	7	12	8
10. Scrubbing	2	1	—	4	1	4	6	2	4
11. Being locked-up	6	—	1	1	—	—	7	—	1

Table 23: *Analysis of the comments made by Werrington and Aylesbury men concerning certain aspects of their training at the detention centres*

	Werrington		Aylesbury		Both	
	Unfavourable	Favourable	Unfavourable	Favourable	Unfavourable	Favourable
1. No smoking	10	—	13	—	23	—
2. Food	8	9	23	3	31	12
3. Early rising; P.T.	20	—	17	8	37	8
4. Physical training (including circuit training)	21	8	5	9	26	17
5. Treatment by officers	12	—	4	4	16	4
6. Strictness; discipline	11	2	3	1	14	3
7. Marching, drill, parades	14	4	9	7	23	11
8. Tempo; lack of leisure	7	—	7	—	14	—
9. Changing	9	—	17	—	26	—
10. Scrubbing	7	1	11	—	18	1
11. Being locked-up	7	2	1	—	8	2

fewer of them had been away from home before (two men gave being away from home as their principal dislike) and fewer have been attuned to penal conditions by experience of prison. Although security measures are far less in evidence at Werrington than at Aylesbury, and it has already been confirmed that some of the Werrington men preferred the detention centre to their experience of prison just for this reason, nevertheless there were still a handful of Werrington men who hated being 'locked-up'.

Superficially at least, the Aylesbury men gave the impression of being more resilient both physically and mentally and of being less affected by the whole treatment process. It is possible that the regime was less arduous for them at this developmental stage. Nevertheless, although the physical and circuit training is made as similar as possible at the centres[10] very few of the Aylesbury men expressed any dislike for it, wanted it changed or suggested that other inmates complained about it. More of them commented unfavourably on marching, which they described as pointless or childish. It was, indeed, any undignified aspects of their training and being treated 'like kids' that they chiefly rejected. They disliked getting up early and doing P.T. but equally they complained of having to change ten times per day which they dismissed as ridiculous. They were also bitter about scrubbing which both at Aylesbury and Werrington was described as 'woman's work'— 'we have our pride, you know'. Several at both centres longed to be out of doors and hated being cooped-up. Two Werrington men thought they ought to be doing constructive work.

There were few strong protests against activities falling outside the eleven main headings. Other criticisms referred to evening classes (9), the association hour (7), kit inspections (4), the beds (1), football (3), having to read (5), the number of letters (2), going to bed so early (3), and going to bed so late (2). Individual men commented unfavourably on the soap, toothpaste, haircuts, loss of remission as a punishment and blunt razor-blades.

When asked if there were any changes they would make, the Aylesbury men were inclined to recommend the removal of the items in the programme that they found irksome and they made suggestions to ease the pressure of the regime—a free afternoon, longer meal-times, more letters, longer time for reading or more

[10]Indeed, during the research period, the physical training instructor was transferred from Werrington to Aylesbury when it opened.

time in the open. The Werrington men also made suggestions under the main headings to make the programme more tolerable but there was an impression that they regarded the unpleasantnesses as inevitable and unchangeable. They, therefore, proposed some constructive additions or modifications such as more schooling, more evening activities, boxing, more field games and the chance to learn a trade.

At both centres the men attributed to others the same sort of complaints as they made themselves. As in every institution, food was apparently the principal topic of discussion. Apart from the complaints of others which fell under the main headings, the Aylesbury men imputed to others some flippant ones which included regrets for the lack of entertainment, leisure and girls.

But at Werrington the adverse comments were said often to centre around the officers. In some of their answers to the three questions, there were allegations of shouting and hitting by officers and criticism of the way in which they sometimes treated the inmates. The Werrington men appeared to be far more concerned than the Aylesbury men with the attitudes and manners of their officers and their relationships with them. This was substantiated by their answers to a direct question concerning the officers:

Table 24: First impressions of these 107 men of their officers at the two detention centres

	Werrington		Aylesbury		Both	
	No.	%	No.	%	No.	%
Majority favourable opinions of officers (e.g. fair, decent, all right etc.)	27	45	28	58	55	52
Mixed opinions (e.g. some fair, some harsh etc.)	14	24	11	23	25	23
Majority adverse opinions (e.g. too strict, nasty, hit, shout etc.)	18	31	9	19	27	25
Totals	59	100	48	100	107	100

The table confirms the fact that more Werrington than Aylesbury men made adverse comments about their officers. However,
slightly more of the Werrington men than of the Aylesbury men
answered in the affirmative to the question 'Do you think it will
be possible to make friends with any of the officers?' which suggests
that the Werrington men may anticipate and hope for closer and
more friendly relationships with the officers, and for this reason
are more easily disappointed. In any case, only 31 per cent. of them
and 27 per cent. of the Aylesbury men thought it might be possible to establish friendly relations. Most of the remainder were sure
it would not be possible to be friendly within the detention centre
regime. A few were uncertain and some said that, although it
might be possible, they would not attempt it. Their reasons were
that, for example, it was not in the nature of the officers' job to
be friendly, that they did not speak in a friendly way, that they
were 'difficult to reach', and that it was not possible to bring them
'personal problems'. Several anticipated being styled a 'creeper'
by other inmates or the officers themselves if they tried to be
friendly.

The men were reserved in discussing the officers but it appears
that the majority of them found most of the officers fair and decent
in the execution of their duties, even if these duties did not foster
friendliness or close relationships. At this stage the Werrington
men who were slightly more often expecting the officers to
be friendly than were the Aylesbury men, alleged that the officers
'shout', 'bawl', 'thump', 'bully them', 'treat them like dirt', 'punch
you in the ribs'; that 'they are moody', 'sometimes they joke but
the next minute they shout at you for being cheeky'; that 'some
think too much of themselves'. A note of condescension entered
into several of the answers of the Aylesbury men. They claimed
that some of the officers 'showed off', that 'you have to understand
them and their moods', 'they are not helpful, but there is no harm
in them', that 'they could be a bit more human', 'one or two are
cocky' and 'you have to be sorry for some of them'. At both centres
there were individual officers who were generally liked and
admired. The reason usually given for liking an officer was that
he was fair, even if strict, and that the men knew where they were
with him. By reason of their job, the physical training instructors
and the reception officers provoked more strong reactions than
most officers being either admired or disliked. The allegations of

68

hitting and 'clipping over the ear' were comparatively few and possibly legendary. Except in two cases of such allegations the men confessed that 'so far' they had not been hit themselves nor had they seen others being hit.

The different reactions of the men at the two centres to the ingredients of their training in the first few days have been demonstrated above.[11] Some of the differences can be attributed to the fact that Werrington was a stable, and from the men's point of view, unchangeable establishment whilst Aylesbury was in a tentative changeable state. Other differences might be evidence of discrepant attitudes to the purpose of the detention centre. Aylesbury inmates appeared to embark upon it as a punitive and deterrent treatment only; the Werrington men may have sought for a reformative, training element. On the other hand, the differences might be not of attitude or reaction but only of response to the interview.[12] It may, in this case, have been the greater honesty and bravado of the more sophisticated Aylesbury men and the simpler conformity and efforts to please of the more uncertain Werrington men, which was reflected in these different answers.

Undeniably the whole training programme, the officers and the first few days' experience of detention were more of an ordeal for the Werrington men than for the Aylesbury men. This difference is further evidenced by the men's answers to the question 'Is there anything about the centre which is better than you thought it would be?' Because fewer of the Werrington men had heard of detention centres before arriving at them, they had only their own general image of penal institutions to judge by and it seemed that nearly half found the centre as bad as they had feared. 40 per cent. of the Aylesbury men, having often heard of Blantyre House or a junior centre, said that the first few days at Aylesbury were better, in most respects, than they expected. Everything was 'less hard'.

The table overleaf indicates the other aspects of the training by which the men were agreeably surprised or which they thought were valuable in any way. Quite a number were pleased

[11]Table 23 (i.e. Analysis of comments made by Werrington and Aylesbury men concerning certain aspects of training.)

[12]As half of each sample were selected at random by each research worker for interview, the differences cannot be attributed to the different reactions to different interviewers.

69

to have physical training and a few actually enjoyed marching and, at Aylesbury, early morning P.T. Other favourable points which they conceded were evening classes (8), kit inspections (7), football (3), reading (3). One Aylesbury man summed up the situation— 'it is only a lot of shouting, it can't hurt you.'

Table 25: Analysis of the answers given by 107 men at Werrington and Aylesbury detention centres to the question 'Is there anything at the centre better than you expected?'

	Werrington	Aylesbury	Both
Nothing better than expected	26	12	38
Everything better or less 'hard' than expected	4	19	23
Physical conditions—i.e. cleanliness, food, comfort, sleeping arrangements better	13	9	22
Had no idea what it would be like	6	1	7
Other factors (games, gym, work, not locked in, discipline)	11	9	20

Initial assessment by the sample of the long-term value of detention centre training

How the men felt about the different facets of their training in this early stage has been considered but greater importance attaches to their assessment of the benefit they will derive from it. They were asked, therefore, whether they thought they were likely to get into further trouble, that is offend again, on their return home.

The answer was almost unanimously 'no'.[13] Those (5) who were almost certain that they would re-offend had circumstances which they thought made further offences inevitable. One man who had committed an assault was convinced he would in the same circumstances be provoked again; another, committed for a series of drunk and disorderly offences, thought he would have further drunkenness charges although he would try not to be caught; a third man said he might steal, if needs be, when the fairgrounds

[13] Approximately nine out of ten men at each centre.

closed down; another, a rootless tramp before he was admitted, in a state of depression and despair since he had been discharged from the army, anticipated further trouble 'unless I get out of the way I feel'. The others who were doubtful about the future said they 'hoped' they would not get into more trouble, they would 'try not to' but they seemed to take little responsibility for whether they did or not. They said, for example, 'I will try but it is difficult to stop', 'I might be one of the ones who come back', and 'the law keeps picking on us'. The others simply said they did not know what might happen.

The reason given for keeping clear of trouble on discharge was in most cases related to the deterrent aspects of the sentence. A little over half at each centre gave as their reasons that they had had 'enough', that they would not want to get sent back to a detention centre, that they realized how stupid they had been, that crime was no good, that they had 'learned their lesson'. Some realized that they would receive more serious treatment next time; others that they did not like being locked up or being away from their friends and families. The remainder hoped that external factors would help. For example, ten had steady girl-friends whom they hoped to marry, three thought that a good job, or change of job, would help, one would stop drinking, two would keep better company. Two men said they would take care not to be caught. In several answers the note of fatalism again entered . . . 'but the law may pin something on me'.

Secondly they were all asked what they would learn at the detention centre that would help them on discharge. On the whole the men did not, at this point, think that there was anything in the detention centre training that would help them to 'go straight' on discharge. Their answers were sometimes confused either with what they had been told they would be taught or what they thought the centre's purpose should be. However, the majority who thought it might be teaching anything saw it again in terms of deterrence, that is, teaching them a lesson by subjecting them to an unpleasant experience or making them realize what they were missing at home.

Table 26: Analysis of answers of 107 Werrington and Aylesbury men to the question 'What do you think you will learn at the detention centre that will help you keep out of trouble (on discharge)'

	Werrington	Aylesbury	Both
Deterrent, 'teaching a lesson'	13	13	26
Discipline, obedience, smartening up	15	9	24
To be 'fit'	4	2	6
To work well	1	5	6
Other points (crafts, getting-up, not smoking, P.T.)	4	4	8
Nothing or 'no idea'	26	15	41

Among those who thought they would learn discipline, obedience and smartness the range was great, from four less delinquent types who thought they would learn to take a pride in themselves and a sense of responsibility, to the men who grudgingly said they 'supposed' they would learn discipline but did not know what use it would be to them outside, particularly when their offence had been a dishonest one. Several men thought the discipline 'ridiculous' as it bore no relation to anything they did outside and claimed they would all have a 'big laugh' when they were discharged. Several quite thoughtful men wondered how the training would help them not to steal, while one man who regarded himself as at the centre for a breach of probation thought discipline might be useful 'in view of his offence'. Several said they already knew all about discipline and smartness. One man said 'they keep calling us tough teddy-boys and coffee-bar bandits and I suppose they are trying to stop us being them but this training will only make us tougher'. At this stage only six men approved of the idea of becoming fit through the physical activities and, indeed, probably few of them thought they ever would. They had almost invariably found their first taste of circuit training and P.T. exacting and frequently complained that they suffered from various disabilities that made them unsuitable for such exertions.

The men's reactions and attitudes to their sentence, to their offences, to their first few days of training and to the future have been described. It appears that in most respects there were clear differences between the men seen at the two detention centres, differences possibly accounted for by geography and criminal sophistication. Generally speaking, however, the men were satisfied to have been sent to detention rather than to any other institutional treatment that they might have been awarded. Some were ambiguous in their answers about prison and might have preferred its comparative idleness but borstal was too long. All of them would probably have preferred to stay at home and many, despite the fact that they had found probation of little value, would have welcomed this alternative and thought they might have been allowed it. The sample was nearly equally divided between those who thought the detention centre the right punishment for them and those who did not, usually because they did not think they needed to be sent away at all. Chiefly they envisage detention as suitable for aggressive, 'tough' types and violent types of offence are, on the whole, the only ones of which they disapprove. Most men were homesick at first when they arrived at the centres but after the first days only a few remained depressed and unhappy. The Werrington men found most parts of the detention centre programme more disagreeable than the Aylesbury men. Few regarded their training as likely to teach them anything except 'not to come back'. They regarded it as an effective deterrent in many cases but it was not necessarily because of this that they were convinced they would not offend again.

Table 27 : *Assessments of the attitudes of the men at Werrington and Aylesbury detention centres after their first few days' experience of the training*

	Werrington		Aylesbury		Both	
	No.	%	No.	%	No.	%
Depressed, miserable, unhappy	13		10		23	
Cocksure, light-hearted, untouched	3	46	6	44	9	45
Resentful, bitter, truculent	11		5		16	
Apparently satisfactory in attitude	32	54	27	56	59	55

The extent to which the men will benefit from their training during the ensuing weeks depends largely on the mood in which they approach it. Table 27 shows an assessment of the men's early attitude to their training as it appeared to the interviewers up to the end of the first interview.

There is, perhaps surprisingly, a close similarity between the proportions at each centre who appeared prepared to accept the sentence which they had to serve and those who, for one reason or another, were less able to do so. The first three assessments were only made where it was believed that the man was depressed, indifferent or resentful enough to affect his reaction and attitude to his training. Over half of the men seemed to the interviewers to be in the right frame of mind to profit from any beneficial aspects of the detention centre regime.

CHAPTER FOUR

THE YOUNG MEN AS THEY APPEARED
TO THE OFFICERS AT THE CENTRES

A VALUABLE contribution to the research programme was made by the prison officers at each centre. Drawing upon their considerable experience with young offenders and, in most cases, with detention centre inmates, they completed a questionnaire in respect of each man in the sample about two weeks before his release from the centre. Because of their experience, they were able to notice individual differences among the men and deviations from the patterns of behaviour and reactions to training that they had come to expect and, because they are in scarcely interrupted contact with the men during training, they are in a position to make detailed observations on their demeanour. To enhance the objectivity of their answers, the questions of the questionnaire were, in most instances, framed on a three-point scale which required the officers to distinguish the exceptional from the average inmate.[1] But, although the detention centre regime does not encourage close personal relationships, the officers are dependent on their personal experience of individual men and to that extent their judgements will inevitably be subjective. However, whether they are mainly subjective or objective, the answers to the questionnaire provide information which links the men's emotionally charged statements concerning their training and its value with the factual evidence of their behaviour seen in the punishments they receive and with the limited proofs of the effects of the training seen in the reconviction and follow-up material. Throughout the training period the officers submit routine reports

[1]As with any such marking system, there is a tendency for the officers to find more exceptions that would be expected in a normally distributed sample, and to give more favourable ratings than might be expected.

on the men, so that their assessments in the questionnaire are dependent on a sustained impression and do not necessarily refer to any specific point in time.

At Werrington four officers completed a questionnaire on each man. These officers included a physical training instructor,[2] two house officers and the officer of the work-party to which the man was attached at the time of the report. At Aylesbury, it was possible for only two officers to report in each case—a physical training instructor and one of the house officers who could also report on the man's work record.

There are, therefore, a number of difficulties implicit in the material which emerges from the answers to the questionnaire and these must be kept in mind in considering the following analysis of these answers. Firstly, it is not possible to make accurate comparisons between the two centres because of the differing number of reporting officers and because confirmation of opinions is less likely or possible with the fewer reporting officers at Aylesbury. In the second place, individual officers have differing standards, and, with the exception of one physical training instructor, no one officer reported on all the men at either centre.

Reactions of the men to their training

The amount of effort made by each man, the alacrity and willingness with which he obeyed orders and the respect or co-operation which he accorded the officers were selected as being symbolic of the men's positive or negative response to their training. These were concepts with which the officers were familiar. They were asked to assess each man on these three training factors by means of the following questions and by using the 'average' detention centre inmate as their criterion for a 'B' answer.

1. EFFORT

    A. Does he make the maximum effort all the time?

    B. Does he make an adequate effort most of the time?

    C. Does he make the minimum effort most of the time?

---

[2]In some cases two P.T.I.'s reported on the Werrington men but as this was not consistent throughout only one P.T.I.'s report has been used for analysis.

2. OBEDIENCE

    A. Does he obey orders and instructions quickly and willingly?
    B. Does he do what is required without getting into trouble?
    C. Does he obey slowly and resentfully?

3. RESPECT AND CO-OPERATION

    A. Is he respectful, co-operative and responsive?
    B. Is he normally co-operative to you?
    C. Is he surly and unco-operative?

The fact that a man is seen as outstanding in any of these training factors, even if it be only by one officer, becomes significant in a regime where the men are spurred on to their maximum endeavour, where instant obedience is demanded and where respect and good manners are expected from men who, in many instances, arrived with a reputation for disorderliness, idleness or anti-social behaviour.

The figures for the two centres cannot be compared, for the reasons previously stated, but there is a similarity in the picture presented of a majority of hard-working, obedient and co-operative inmates. Not many men qualify for an assessment of outstanding effort whereas the majority at each centre are thought by at least one officer to display respect and co-operation and, at Werrington, to be willing and obedient. The Aylesbury sample has only about one-third who are regarded as willingly obedient; a quarter of them were reluctantly obedient.

In Table 28 an attempt is made to isolate the nucleus of good and poor trainees at each centre. Those men who received a mixture of good and poor assessments are regarded as unclassifiable for the purpose of this table. There are only five men at each centre who are noticeably poorer trainees although there is some evidence from later answers that the average and unclassifiable groups contain a proportion of men who, in other respects, might be considered rather poor trainees.

Four of the Werrington group will serve as examples of those considered by the reporting officers to be very good trainees. Each of these received nine or more 'A' assessments on the three training factors. One was at the centre for driving whilst disqualified (—this group had the best record for the training factors). He was bright, competent and assured and was annoyed at finding himself at the detention centre both because of the nature of his offence and because he had been the mainstay at home since his father's death. Nevertheless, he clearly inspired confidence and was, in the officers' opinion, the most outstanding man of the sample. One had taken and driven away a vehicle.[3] This offender was a very fat man who was passionately keen on cars. He behaved naturally and competently in the detention centre setting, giving the impression of having good sense and humour. He was allotted a responsible job which brought him into more contact with the officers than was the case with most men. The third of this group of four was one of the violent offenders, although he was not

Table 28: Men of the sample grouped according to the number of good (A) average (B) and poor (C) assessments they received from the officers for their effort, obedience and respect in training

	Werrington	Aylesbury	Both
Very Good Trainees			
Majority 'A' assessments	8	2	10
Good Trainees			
Werrington: 4-6 'A' assessments			
Aylesbury: 2-3 'A' assessments	15	12	27
Average Trainees			
Majority 'B' assessments	15	21	36
Poor Trainees			
Werrington: 4-6 'C' assessments			
Aylesbury: 2-3 'C' assessments	4	3	7
Very Poor Trainees			
Majority 'C' assessments	1	2	3
Unclassifiable			
Some 'A', 'B' and 'C' assessments	12	6	18
Total	55	46	101

typical of them.[4] This was the young man who had been committed for assaulting his step-father. Although he came from a highly delinquent neighbourhood he had remained free from con-

[3]This group of offenders also has several of the best trainees but over half are average and two poor.

[4]A proportion of the violent offenders did do well in training, but they had among their small numbers, three of the poorest performers.

victions until this time. He was hurt and depressed by the sentence of the court but from the outset of his training he accepted it in a resigned way. His home life was difficult so that he may not have found the detention centre as unpleasant as some inmates with more indulgent homes. One reason for his difficulties with his step-father had been that he could not obtain employment but he was said, at the end of his training, to be able to do a good day's work. He was also good at all physical activities. It seemed at the end of his detention that he had become hardened and he claimed friendship with several of the more delinquent men from his area but he remained unidentified with criminal behaviour and remarked that he would not want to mix with people who 'screwed' cars. The last of the four was a representative of the largest and most assorted group of dishonest offenders. This man was a happy-go-lucky, foot-loose Irishman with only one offence of drunkenness prior to his current offence of stealing records and a record player in a drunken melee. He had the customary charm of the Irishman and after some initial resentment at losing his freedom took his training in good part. He had led a gay life and deprivation of liberty irked him but he was probably other-wise little affected by this experience of detention. After his six months sentence he claimed only to have learned to 'look after himself'. He was well aware that he had created a good impression and was proud of having acquired one of the more 'cushy' jobs at the centre. Seven months after his release from the centre he was heavily fined for a taking and driving away offence.

At Aylesbury, with the limited number of reporting officers, there are only two very good trainees distinguishable. One of these, was a young married man, more mature than many inmates. He had been a youth club leader and managed to put on a front of great conformity and co-operation but he may not have been as law-abiding and well-intentioned as he led everyone to believe. The other was also more mature and sophisticated than many.

At the other end of the scale are the ten poor trainees. Three of these had been committed for assaults and in two cases had been very resentful on admission. One of these was a slightly coloured youth whose difficulties appeared to stem from this and other factors relating to his position in the family. Another violent offender was an aggressive but serious-minded man who had only one previous offence and had stayed in one job for five years. He was strongly individual and mature and probably kicked against the restrictions of the centre. None of these three violent offenders had serious records of previous offences but some of the poor trainees had. Two were ex-approved schoolboys and another had a history of many offences of disorderliness and troublesome behaviour. His record showed only one earlier serious offence in addition to his current one of breaking and entering but throughout his training he seemed destined to be in minor trouble. He was distressed by the punishments he received, admitted that they were deserved but did not appreciate that he could do anything to improve his situation. It is significant that he is one of the few men who were assessed by a majority of officers as being 'stupid or dim', especially as he left school from the 'A' stream and was given a good report by his headmaster.

The two worst trainees at Aylesbury consisted of a youth who had already spent three months in a junior detention centre. He was happy-go-lucky about the whole experience saying that he found it all easier at the senior centre. He was said by one of the officers to have deteriorated during training and certainly he seemed as immature and inconsequential when he left as when he arrived although he claimed to have sorted out some of his home problems in the meantime. The other appeared tearful, weak and homesick on first interview and came from a normal home, although there appeared to have been some friction between the man and his father. He said that as he had been caught he must 'take his punishment' but tended to blame others for his defections and to excuse himself. He received a poor report from an attendance centre who reported that he 'detested P.T., was pathetic at all activities, refused to be guided yet nevertheless he had completed the order satisfactorily'. At the detention centre he was said to be 'childish and to laugh at little things'. He received extra work for laughing at an officer but despite his very poor record at the centre he did not lose any remission.

Representative of those who caused disagreement among the officers were two of the men who completed shorter terms of detention as a result of non-payment of fines. Both were older than most inmates. One, after two months at the centre, was thought by three officers to have remained unaffected by his training and, by one, to have made the minimum of effort throughout. On the other hand, one officer had found him co-operative and respect-

ful and thought he had a good chance of success in the future
while another said 'he bends with the wind and it is doubtful
whether the treatment will have any lasting effect'. This and the
man's own statement that he had not been changed by detention
have been proved true by his re-conviction within three months
of discharge from the centre and his committal to borstal training.
The other man also completed two months. He was mature but
irresponsible and slovenly in speech and manner. Yet, although
he gave the impression of sloppiness, he was not only good at P.T.
but also set in his ways and unlikely to be affected by his training.
Two officers assessed him as lacking in effort; two found him above
average in obedience and respect. Although he seemed unchanged
at the end of his training there is no news of his reconviction.
A tiresome, irresponsible younger man also caused disagreement,
but chiefly because he responded well at his work and yet was a
nuisance in other respects. Several who fall into this indeterminate
category do so because one officer, in the face of one or more
favourable assessments from others, found the man disrespectful.
This may be indicative of the personal and subjective nature of
such assessments.

Although the violent offenders produce proportionately the
most poor trainees and the fewest good ones, it is the older age
groups, to which they frequently belong, that do best in their
training. The young seventeen-year olds do less well than others.
Three out of every five take and drive away offender is in this
youngest age-group.

The spirit in which the men embarked upon their training does
not appear greatly to affect their performance in training,
although those who appeared to have satisfactory attitudes[5]
towards it, have the largest proportion of good trainees. The few
poor trainees are more evenly divided among the three groups of
men with cocksure, resentful and satisfactory attitudes but the
miserable and depressed men had only one poor trainee among
them. There may be some significance in the fact that three out
of the small group of 'cocksure' men (8) cause disagreement
among the officers and all three have been reconvicted within six
months of their discharge from the centre.

The men's attitudes to their training emerged in their answers
to other questions of the initial interview. For example, they were

[5]See Chapter III, p. 73.

asked whether they thought they had been awarded the right sentence and over half replied that they did not think they had. It seemed probable that those who did not think that detention was the right punishment for themselves would make less good trainees than others who accepted it. When the answers are related to the training assessments, it appears that this is the case. Only two of those who admitted it was probably the right treatment made poor trainees. However, a number (7) of those who were good trainees had rejected the punishment as unsuitable for themselves.

Another question which was asked at the first interview and which was thought likely to have some bearing on the men's reaction to training was what they thought they were likely to learn from detention. In Table 26, Chapter III, it was seen that many men did not see any point in their training, some regarded it as deterrent only and a number thought they might derive something positive from it (fitness, discipline, a taste for hard work, etc.). In this case, if the replies to the question are related to good and poor performance in training it becomes evident that the men who see positive possibilities in their training do no better than those who think the training will be pointless. Those who regard the training as deterrent only are not generally outstanding, while those who discount the value of it, on the whole, do best.

It has been suggested that personal attitudes will inevitably enter into the officers assessments of the men in training. It would equally be expected that the attitudes of individual men to the officers both collectively and individually would influence their performance during training and the rating they receive for their behaviour. This hypothesis, too, appears partially incorrect. The men who in Table 24, Chapter III, alleged that they had found most of the officers fair and decent have, indeed, among them more good trainees but also more poor trainees than those who either disliked all or some of them. Similarly, the men who think it might be possible to make friends with the officers do no better in terms of the training factors than those who rule this possibility out.

Only twelve men at the first interview anticipated further trouble when they were released from the centre. Three of this group proved good trainees but the trouble they anticipated was in each case due to personal circumstances that they felt they could not control. Only two proved poor trainees.

82

This evidence seems to suggest that the early attitudes of the men to their training have only limited relevance to their behaviour in training as observed by the officers. The fact that the answers to the question whether detention was the right punishment have a positive relationship with good and poor performance in training, whereas early attitudes to the officers and to the benefit to be derived from detention have little relationship with the same training factors, may also reflect a difference of response by the men to different types of question. They are forced to make a personal judgement about the rightness of the punishment for themselves but, to the other questions, they could make stereotyped responses derived from what they have been told or heard discussed. For the normal adolescent who tends to reject authority and its symbols it is probably more natural to say he will learn nothing from detention and that he hates all the officers but this in no way prevents him, after his protest, from settling well to the training and developing satisfactory relationships.

It may eventually be possible to establish whether the way in which a man behaves during training has any bearing on his ultimate adjustment to life in the community. In the meantime, answers to further questions of the questionnaire shed light on who the men were whom the officers regarded as good, average or poor trainees.

A-typical inmates

The majority of men (70 per cent.) were thought to correspond to the image of the average detention centre inmate that the officers had created for themselves. Thirty-one men were thought by one or more officers to be a-typical in some respect but, of these, nineteen were apparently unusual because they displayed qualities superior to other inmates and twelve were different for less favourable reasons. Because the majority group of average or typical men is so heterogeneous, the officers' concept of the typical inmate can more readily be derived from considering those they regard as a-typical. The favourable comments included references to maturity, self-confidence, better upbringing, good manners, a more intelligent outlook, realization of stupidity, lack of resentment or self-pity, used to discipline, a good sportsman, always helpful and co-operative, not 'loud-mouthed', and several allusions to quietness, timidity, and in-offensiveness. For example, the one asthmatic young man was said to be 'more to be pitied than blamed' and 'that he would not hurt a fly' and the man who assaulted his step-father was thought unusual because he was 'very quiet, nothing flustered or annoyed him and he took everything in his stride'. One deprived, unhappy first offender who found the whole experience of detention very frightening was said to be unlike others because he was 'not a criminal type'. It is interesting that the man with a 'better upbringing' was brought up exclusively in large Children's Homes until the age of fifteen when he had been placed in lodgings and that the man who was 'used to discipline' was reported as having an unsympathetic and over-strict father.

The twelve unfavourable reasons for a-typicalness were chiefly concerned with criminality. One man was described as a baby-faced thug, another as a younger version of Dartmoor-type inmate. Other officers said of individual men 'he wants to be a leader among hooligans and thugs', 'he makes criminals his idols' and 'he is a con-man in the making' and of others, that they were too resentful and aggressive or that they were 'hard cases'. Only one man was thought unusual because he was 'more backward than most'. Similarly, although there were fourteen men in the sample who had shown some signs of instability and who had been referred to psychiatrists, mental hospitals or clinics for some reason and although five of this group were among those regarded as 'a-typical', only one of these were judged unusual because of this instability. This man was unable to tell the truth, indulged in fantasy and was reported by one officer to 'talk himself into trouble' and by another to 'know too much and to be argumentative and a liar'. Another strange and resentful man with no recorded history of instability was said to be 'hard to understand, deep and moody'. He gave a similar impression on interview when he alleged that he was unable to remember many simple personal details. He clearly expected the world to be against him and said of one of the officers that he was 'fair and decent but he doesn't like me'. However, it is possible that this young man was no more than dull and slow-witted.

From their comments it might be deduced that the officers regard the typical detention centre inmate as immature, badly brought up, ill-mannered, uncertain, stupid, self-pitying, resentful, often loud-mouthed, sometimes bumptious and tiresome, but not

very tough or aggressive, not a 'thug' and not well-established
in criminal ways or outlook. Rather obviously all those who were
judged a-typical because of their good qualities made average or
better trainees except three who received conflicting training
assessments. Similarly, all those who were deemed a-typical because
of their defects, made only average or worse trainees, with the exception, again, of one man who received contradictory training
assessments—the man who made criminals his idols. He was
generally recognized as being a poor prospect and was, indeed,
reconvicted soon after release, but he was a quick bright youth
who did not do too badly in training.

Criminality of inmates

Although criminality appears to be one of the grounds upon which
the officers regard men as typical or not, there are a number of
men who are not thought to be unusual and yet, in answer
to another question, are thought to be 'criminal in outlook' rather
than 'only mildly delinquent'. There are, in fact, nineteen men
at each centre who are so assessed and only thirteen of this total
of thirty-eight are among the a-typical group, and in several cases
for quite other reasons. Fifteen of the total were said by more than
one officer to be criminal rather than delinquent. It is difficult to
assess to what extent the judgement of the officers is influenced
by what they have learned of the men's histories. However, when
an attempt is made to find out who these so-called criminal types
are, it appears they include a higher proportion of offenders with
more than four offences, a higher proportion of those with recent
rather than longer criminal records, and all but one of the ex-
approved schoolboys. They also include all those with poor or
very poor training assessments and only four of the good trainees,
two of whom were thought by two officers to be criminal.

Too much weight must not be attached to any relationships
which exist between criminality and behaviour in training as seen
by the officers, because the man who does badly in training may,
for that reason alone, be thought of as incorrigible and have
criminality imputed to him. This seems to be confirmed by the fact
that the actual criminal records of the men—that is, the number
of previous offences, the length of record and the incidence of
institutional treatment—seem to have little relevance to whether

85

the man makes a good or poor trainee. Offenders who had taken and driven away vehicles were more often good trainees than those who had committed offences of violence but it is the former who are more often assessed as criminal in outlook. This may be because taking and driving away is known to be a recidivist offence whereas violence may be recognized as more likely to be an isolated offence, despite its unacceptability and the aggressiveness and unco-operativeness of these offenders at the centre. But if the offence is being taken into consideration by the officers when they assess criminality, it is surprising that the larger and heterogeneous group of dishonest offenders are not more often considered criminal.

But the officers have opportunities to overhear the men talking among themselves and to watch the influences operating among the group. Thus, it may be something independent of behaviour in training that they are conscious of when they assess criminality. Later it will be seen that a larger proportion of those deemed criminal in outlook than of those who were assessed as poor, average or unclassifiable trainees, had been reconvicted within six months of release from the centre.

Intelligence shown during training

The chance of a man adjusting to life in the detention centre or life in the community may be greater or less according to his endowment of intelligence and the level at which he manages to function. It has been shown in Chapter II that there are few men in the sample who show evidence of being above average in intelligence. At the lower end of the scale, four boys had attended schools for the educationally sub-normal, but ten others functioned at a low level (i.e. had low intelligence quotients, were illiterate or attended special classes for the dull). The officers, when asked to place the men on a three-point scale for their intelligence, thought twenty-three men more intelligent than the average and twenty-two men less intelligent. These were, of course, in many cases, the opinions of single officers. They included only about half of those known to be dull or more intelligent.

According to the officers' assessments, the bright men make good trainees with only two exceptions where intelligence appeared to be synonymous with cunning. The officers' dull and stupid men were usually average or poor trainees except five who did well despite the supposed handicap (two of these were known dullards). For the officers, good intelligence in this context is good sense in the training situation and low intelligence is, for them, equivalent to stupidity and unexplained tiresomeness of behaviour.

But if intelligence, insofar as it can be judged by the man's educational records or intelligence test results, is compared with the training assessments, it is found that the men with low intelligence do slightly better than either those with evidence of higher intelligence or the sample as a whole. It is probably not surprising that among those assessed by the officers as average or adequate in intelligence there should be a number who, outside the detention centre setting, had not only shown evidence of dullness, but also often had difficulties on that account, for the regime at the centre is simple and the routine undemanding in terms of comprehension. Several of the dull men had, in any case, already undergone some institutional treatment and could, therefore, do what was required without being commented upon for their stupidity. Dullness does not appear necessarily to be a handicap in training nor high intelligence an advantage but an air of good sense and responsibility clearly inspire confidence. Bewilderment and stupidity either elicit sympathetic treatment or adverse comments.

Physical ability of inmates

Since physical activities form a considerable part of the training programme it might have been expected that the physically incompetent youth would be noticed as unusual on this account. But, again, there was only one who was regarded as a-typical, and at a disadvantage because of his physical disability. This was the asthmatic young man who received remedial treatment at the centre from which he benefited. The physical training instructors assessed the men's ability at physical activities on a three-point scale. In this case, as there is only one officer reporting at each centre, the figure for the two centres can be compared.

It was shown in Chapter III[6] that the Werrington men more often complained about the physical activities than their Aylesbury counterparts did. This may partly be accounted for by the

[6]See Chapter III, p.63.

cases did the officers think a man was unpopular or unacceptable and, in all but one instance, this was the opinion of a single officer. The exception was the unstable, untruthful man committed for indecent exposure. Nearly half the sample were thought by at least one officer to be popular and these opinions were confirmed by more than one officer in over a third of the cases. There appears to be no great difference in the way in which the officers regard the behaviour in training of the two groups of popular and unpopular men, although the former have a better proportion of good trainees. It may be significant that five of the allegedly unpopular men fall into the unclassifiable category. There is, in fact, an indication that unpopularity stems from eccentric behaviour, dullness or physical unattractiveness. Two of the group had committed sexual offences (but, equally, two other sexual offenders were assessed as being popular). On the other hand, there are one or two who appear to be good trainees and who are unpopular because they think themselves more mature than others and, therefore, seem impatient and even arrogant.

Those who are regarded as popular are in most cases good trainees and, indeed, eight out of the total (10) of very good trainees are observed as being popular by two or more officers. It appears that there is no ostracism in these cases for what might be regarded as over-conformity.[7] But those who have previous institutional experience, those who were regarded as criminal in outlook by the officers, and those who are serving six-month sentences also had more than the average proportion of popular men. Some of these were clearly liked and admired for their sophistication and experience like the ex-approved schoolboy whom three officers observed as being popular. He had experienced three approved schools, committed offences of several categories, was paying maintenance for an illegitimate child, and frequented drinking clubs and haunts of known adult criminals. Yet, although he was dull in intelligence, he was good at physical activities and managed, at the detention centre, to convey the impression of obedience and respect without effort. It is perhaps interesting that this young man, eighteen months previously, had been transferred to a mental hospital from his approved school

[7]But on the other hand, the officers may have been biased in their impression and assessment of the popularity of the co-operative trainees.

because of his agressive and difficult behaviour towards other inmates.

It looks as though it is the competent, co-operative trainee or the sophisticated, more experienced inmate who is observed by the officers as being popular and, thus, influential over his associates. An allusion is made in the following chapter to the racial prejudices of some of the men in the group. It is interesting that there were two partially coloured men among them neither of whom were allegedly unpopular with the rest. It is the one pathetic but unattractive Jewish boy who is the only one who might have his unpopularity attributed to prejudice. The type of regime at the detention centre, where there is little time or place for close friendships to develop, probably suits the man who finds it difficult to make lasting relationships with his peers, so that it is only the arrogant individualist or the weak eccentric who is represented among the few who were thought by the officers to be unacceptable to their group.

Results of training

The officers had three final questions to consider: had the man improved as a result of his training; was he ready for discharge now; and would he remain free from serious trouble after his release?

Half of the sample were thought by a majority of their officers to have improved as a result of their training and only thirteen seemed, to a majority of the reporting officers, to have remained the same despite it. The improved men were, in fact, those who had been good trainees and the unaffected men were, with few exceptions, those who had been average or poor trainees. One notable exception was the man who had several previous offences and had already, just before his seventeenth birthday, spent three months in a junior centre yet was thought by the officers to be likely to keep out of trouble on discharge. His previous sentence had not, it appears, deterred him, so that it must have been on his good showing at the detention centre, where he had the advantage of knowing what was expected of him, that the officers based their optimism.

Conversely, there was one man who was one of the worst trainees but was, nevertheless, thought to have improved by a majority of the officers. He was one of those regarded by the officers as below average in intelligence.

That nearly half the men who had not improved fall into the classification of average trainees adds further weight to the theory that this group contains more of the less good trainees than their training assessments indicate.

As might be expected there were only three men who were said by the officers to have deteriorated during their training. One is the very immature 'baby' at his centre who was anxious to be one of the more sophisticated group. He was a dull man who could have been easily led. Another is a youth who appeared, at least, un-affected by his second sentence of detention and the third was a first offender. He had been rejected by his father who had remarried and he had spent much time in a school for maladjusted children followed by an aimless existence in residential employment, living on the fringe of prostitute and delinquent society. By the end of his detention he appeared anxious to be counted among the more deeply delinquent types, using their jargon and boasting of what he might or might not do in the future and rather proudly claiming that the officers had given him up as one of the ones who were irredeemable.

Those the officers think are ready for discharge at the end of their training (forty-seven have such ratings confirmed by more than one officer) are also the good trainees while those they think require longer or different treatment (nineteen have confirmed ratings) are poorer trainees. A few (12) good trainees were thought to have been ready for discharge earlier than the end of their sentence. Three of these had served a six-months' sentence but five others who served these longer sentences were nevertheless thought still to need longer. Each of the men who had completed shorter orders of one or two months were assessed by at least one officer as requiring longer.

The officers were asked to predict, from their knowledge of each man, whether the man's chances of keeping out of serious trouble were good, moderate or poor. The difficulty of the uneven number of officers at Werrington and Aylesbury is again encountered and, once again, the results from Werrington are more interesting because of the greater possibilities of agreement. Table 30 shows the distribution of the men according to the combined prognoses of all their officers on a five-point scale.

to the Officers at the Centres

There is a close relationship between the officers' predictions and their assessments of the training factors and the same relationship exists between training factors and improvement in training or readiness for discharge. These results would seem to indicate that the officers assume either that those who respond well during training will benefit as a result of it and thus do well in the future, or that it is the less delinquent and unruly who become good trainees and at no time would they have been considered likely recidivists.

Table 30: Prognostic ratings given by the officers to the men at Werrington and Aylesbury*

	Werrington No.	Werrington %	Aylesbury No.	Aylesbury %
A. Majority of *good* ratings	7	13	4	9
B. Equal *good* and moderate ratings	13	24	15	33
C. Majority of *moderate* ratings	16	29	9	20
D. Equal *poor* and moderate ratings	3	5	10	21
E. Majority *poor* ratings	5	9	7	15
X. Mixed good, poor and moderate	11	20	1	2
All	55	100	46	100

* There are eleven men in the Werrington sample and one among the Aylesbury men who cannot be included in the progressive scale because they received mixed good, moderate and poor ratings.

In fact, those with four or more previous proved offences receive less good prognoses than those with fewer previous offences although there are three of these who qualify for an 'A' prognosis. The six ex-Approved school boys received three 'E' prognosis, two 'X' ratings implying rather natural doubts and one 'A'. The four ex-junior detention centre boys received assorted prognoses with an 'A' assessment going to the man who performed well at the centre but who has already been quoted for the fact that he was said to have remained the same despite his training.

Those who have taken and driven away vehicles seem to be allotted the highest proportion of unsatisfactory prognoses. They are followed by the violent offenders. The disqualified drivers have all good or moderate ratings, which might be expected, but it is

93

again surprising that the dishonest offenders are, comparatively, not considered to be bad risks.

The value of the answers to the officers' questionnaire seems to be intrinsic and to lie chiefly in the picture that is presented through the officers of the inmates of a detention centre as a whole and the individuals of the sample in particular. Considerable individual differences are observed by the officers and the fact that certain officers see certain men differently and, indeed, sometimes contradictorily, indicates that each man is being observed as an individual. The impression gained in this chapter of a collection of distinctive individuals, for whom there seems to be no prototype and few common attributes, confirms this. That there is room for individualized treatment is shown by the sympathetic treatment afforded to some very dull or unstable men. But if the assessment of dullness or instability is as subjective as is suggested in this chapter, there are possibilities of poor behaviour and incompetence being attributed to the wrong motives and of real disabilities failing to be recognized. On the other hand, there are advantages in all men being given standardized treatment unprejudiced by consideration of past records, behaviour and stability. In any case, there is evidence in the material that the man's record of behaviour outside and his attitudes to his sentence have little relevance to his overt behaviour in training. This is particularly noticeable with those who are 'institutionally-sophisticated'—the ex-Approved school boy, the man brought up in Children's homes and those who have already completed a junior detention centre order.

The question remains whether the men will, on release, return to the attitudes of their pre-training days or whether they will carry some elements of their behaviour and attitudes in training with them into the community. The extent to which changes and modifications in attitude occur during the process of training is discussed in the following chapter.

CHAPTER FIVE

THE SECOND INTERVIEW

SEVERAL circumstances combined to make the second interview with these young men easier and more relaxed than the
first. The interviewers were themselves more accustomed to the
centres in which the interviews took place; they were more at ease
with the staff and more aware of the problems and difficulties surrounding the execution of a sentence of detention. They were able
to recognize the men as they entered the room and to anticipate
the weaknesses of understanding and vocabulary that made some
of the previous interviews painful. The men too were more at
ease. They expected recognition and understood or at least
accepted the purpose of a further enquiry into their attitudes. Since
their date of release was near they were, on the whole, cheerful
and excited, so that the atmosphere of the interview was friendly
and answers more readily obtained. It is true also that the questions that were being asked were straightforward and more easily
understood.

Plans for discharge and subsequent employment

The first series of questions related to the man's release, where he
was going, did he have a job to go to, what did he intend to do on
his first night home? These questions were put to the men at the
beginning of the second interview because it was anticipated that
the thought of their discharge would dominate the men's account
of their response to the sentence. This was, in fact, true. Every
answer and every observation was coloured by the knowledge that
in a day or two all the hardships of the centre would be over and
they would be free.

At the beginning of their sentence, the men who had remained
at home up to the time of their offence had looked back on their

life and, in more than one case out of every three, reported discord and difficulty beyond the normal.[1] As they looked forward to their discharge eighty-five out of the group of 101 men said that they were returning to what they looked on as their home. Some of them were aware of the difficulties they would be likely to encounter but they could think of no alternative, since nearly 70 per cent. of them knew that they had no work to go to and nearly all of them had little money. Of the sixteen who were not returning home, six had made arrangements to stay with the families of their girl-friends, married brothers or sisters, adoptive parents and so on. Nine had nowhere to go. Of these two were Irish immigrants who did not wish to return to their families in Ireland but the rest had been rejected by their families or were unable to return because there was no accommodation. Two families were being evicted and another had already been broken up because the mother and some of the children had been forced to accept Part III accommodation.[2] There was no father.

It was clear that there were other difficulties which worried some of the men as they considered their resumption of normal life. Two men who came from respectable homes were disturbed about their reception outside, what their friends and neighbours would think of them, how people would behave towards them and whether they should attempt to conceal the fact of their sentence. There was anxiety too about further court appearances which were known to be impending, and the attitude of the police towards them after a period 'inside'.

The uncertainty which sometimes lay beneath the men's good spirits at this point in their sentence was most marked in their attitude to the prospects of finding work when they were discharged. There is no doubt that they now regarded this as a first priority, partly because of the frustration many of them felt when they received only 1/6d for a hard week's work. They knew that the same amount of work outside would earn for them a considerable wage and they were eager to have it. Many of them however would have to start afresh in whatever job they could find. In answer to the question 'Have you a job to go to?' Sixty-

[1] Chapter II, p. 35.

[2] Accommodation of a very basic kind provided by Local Authorities for families evicted from their homes or otherwise in need. Families are usually split up so as to separate the adult males when such housing is provided.

four men said they had not. Thirty-four of these (74 per cent.) were at the Aylesbury Centre and thirty (55 per cent.) were at Werrington.

Thus more than six out of every ten men leaving both centres knew that they were faced with unemployment for a short time at least. The position was worse for men leaving the Aylesbury centre but this is probably because more of the Aylesbury men were unemployed at the time of the offence for which they were sentenced to detention.[3]

Bad as the situation appeared to the offenders to be, the interviewers were aware that the true position was even worse since several of the men who thought they were returning to their old employment would not in fact be able to do so. The reports of the employers which were available in the files showed that six of them would not re-employ the men, not necessarily because they were bad workmen but because their jobs were filled or the employers felt that the men were unreliable. Thus only three out of every ten men would return to work which was familiar to him or assured through the good offices of probation officers and parents.

Those who knew they had to find work approached the task in varying moods. Most of them recognized their own responsibilities in the matter and said they would go to the Labour Exchange to try to find a job that would suit them, others said they would just 'look around'. One or two were very anxious and made repeated enquiries about how they could find work after a period 'inside'. A few said they would not look for work at once, they would wait until they had recovered from their sentence. One man said he did not intend to work at all. He had a plan for setting up a book-maker's business with the small capital of a friend of his who had been left a legacy. There was no evidence about how firm this arrangement was and no reply was received to the follow-up enquiry in this case.

Although the first series of questions about their homes and their work must have made the men realize, however dimly, that life outside the centre would present serious problems to them, they turned with enthusiasm to consider the next three questions which concerned their immediate satisfactions on release. What

[3]Chapter II, p. 40.

are you looking forward to most? What have you missed most?
And what are you going to do on your first night home? The
answer to the first question was given without hesitation for the
men had been talking and thinking of their release since the
moment of their entry. The answer to the second question was
often an extension or a repetition of the first. The following table
combining the answers to the first two questions shows the
deprivations which had been most keenly felt during the sentence
and so indicates the nature of the punishment inflicted by
a detention centre sentence.

*Table 31 : Answers given to the questions. What are you looking forward to
most and what have you missed most ?**

	Werrington	Aylesbury	Total
Being free	23	26	49
Smoking	19	23	42
Going home or being at home	25	14	39
Girl-friends or girls	10	15	25
Friends, dancing, cinema	6	15	21
Drinking	9	7	16

*This table has been compiled by counting the number of times different
men said that they had been looking forward to or had missed some particular item e.g. dancing, smoking etc. The differences revealed between the
Aylesbury and Werrington groups are greater than they seem since the
number of men interviewed at Werrington was 55 and at Aylesbury it
was 46.

There were some answers that may have been frivolous or may
have reflected an irritation that was increased by the loss of
freedom. One man, for example, said he looked forward to having
sugar in his tea, another to eating fruit again, while a third said
he missed his dog most of all, but this last response was probably
a crude attempt to win the sympathy of the interviewer.

To the men at Werrington and at Aylesbury the principal
element in the detention centre sentence was the loss of freedom.
Although this was expressed more frequently by the men at the
Aylesbury centre it may only be a reflection of the greater power of

expression of the southerners.[4] The Aylesbury group also seemed to suffer more from the no-smoking rule although they broke it more often, mainly because, in the early days of the centre when strict supervision was not possible through lack of staff, cigarettes were smuggled in at visiting times and distributed among the men. One man at this centre said that his greatest deprivation was not that he could not smoke, but that he could not smoke openly. Going home or being at home comes only third in the order of priorities when the whole group is being considered. Once again, however, the difference between the Aylesbury and the Werrington group is observed. Men from Werrington put their desire to be at home before anything else. To the sophisticated men at Aylesbury it comes very nearly last. Surprisingly, drinking does not seem to be important to these young men as they consider the deprivations of the centre itself. Perhaps it is included under the more general heading of freedom, since, in answer to the question 'What will you do the first night home?' many of the men replied that they would go out for a drink.

Table 32 gives a general indication of the plans the men were making for the first evening after their release. The importance of the factor of drinking or drunkenness has already been pointed out in connection with offences of taking and driving and violence.[5] One half of those who committed these offences was found to have done so as a result of drinking too much. In the final interview ten of the thirty-six men found guilty of violence or taking and driving said they would spend their first evening drinking, either alone or with friends. The others said they would stay at home or go out with their girl-friends.

There is a clear contrast between the immediate plans of the men at the two centres. Those who came from the Midlands and the north and who were serving their sentence at Werrington showed less desire to seek out their friends as soon as they were

[4]The Aylesbury men described what they meant by freedom. 'Walking about without an officer with a bunch of keys at your back.' 'Not having to say, yes sir, no sir, all the time', 'being treated like men, not kids' 'not being locked up'. The men from Werrington generally had one picture in their minds 'walking up the drive and getting on to a bus'. This greater uniformity of response was probably due to the fact that the drive leading to a bus stop and freedom was constantly before the eyes of the men as they worked about the garden and farm.

[5]Chapter II, p.41.

Table 32: Answers to the question 'What are you going to do on your first night home?'

	Werrington	Aylesbury	Total
Go out for a drink	9	19	28
Go out and meet the boys	3	9	12
See girl-friend	9	9	18
Stay at home	17	7	24
Go out with parents, go and see friends of family	5	4	9
Go to a dance-hall	3	3	6
Go to a cinema	3	2	5
Go to a youth club	2	—	2
Go away for a weekend	—	1	1
Has no money to do anything	—	1	1
Don't know	5	3	8

The number of those who would spend some part of their first evening in a pub is greater than the 28 who give the answer since those who were going to look for their mates would often find them there. A few, who were going to see their girl-friends said they would probably go and have a drink together. In some cases there appeared to be a deliberate intention to get drunk. One man said he intended to 'get paralytic', a few more said they were looking forward to a 'booze up'. One, who was involved in offences of dishonesty with two others also at the centre said he was going to meet others 'for a good drink'. He has since been reconvicted.

There are more answers than men in this table because some men gave more than one answer.

discharged. Their thoughts, as expressed to the interviewers, were more concentrated on going home and staying home. This is consistent with the answers given to the questions 'What have you missed most and what are you looking forward to most?' that have been analysed in Table 31. There too the men from Werrington showed that their family ties were stronger than those of the men at Aylesbury.

When the men were classified in accordance with the offences for which they were sent to the centre there was no marked difference in their plans for the first night of freedom save in one small respect. Four out of the seven offenders found guilty of driving while disqualified said they would stay at home with their families. The numbers are too small for any conclusion but the impression already gained that the disqualified drivers formed a law-abiding and even orthodox group, is confirmed in this small matter of the men's plans for their first night of freedom.

General impressions of the centres

When they were seen for a second time, the men summed up their impressions of the centres to which they were committed by answering the following three questions :

(1) What would you tell a friend about the detention centre regime?
(2) What would you most dislike to come back to?
(3) What reasons would you give for avoiding being sent to a centre?

In three cases the men said they would not describe the centre to anyone. Two would pretend they had not been there, the third would try to forget all about it. Nothing would persuade these men to answer the question. Generally, however, there was enough information to provide a clear picture of the men's reactions to the whole regime. Table 33[6] is compiled from the answers to these three questions. Comparative figures are given for answers to a similar question at the earlier interview. It shows, therefore, those elements in the detention centre rules and regimen which roused unfavourable comment among the men at the beginning and at the end of their sentence.

It is noticeable that the actual number of unfavourable comments has declined but not in every item listed. The most marked changes occur in the items, food; changing, physical training and circuit training, early morning physical training; marching and games. The complaints about food, it has been noted,[7] were not all groundless since at the Aylesbury centre there were serious shortages for a time. When food was plentiful there were few complaints.

Considering together the items early rising, physical training, marching and changing, it is possible to discern a marked reduc-

---

[6]Favourable comments have been omitted in this table because the questions to which these comments are the answers pre-supposed some unfavourable reactions. Some favourable remarks were however made, especially about physical training and circuit training.

[7]Chapter III, p.63.

tion in the dislike and even hatred with which the men at first regarded the physical exertions to which they were subjected on their first arrival at the centre. The change in the attitude of the Aylesbury group to early rising and repeated changing of clothes may be attributed, in part, to the time of year at which the sentence was served, since the second interviews with these men were conducted in the fine weather of early summer. Even the Werrington

Table 33: Unfavourable comments made by the men on the rules and restrictions of the two centres. Figures are given to show the differences between the comments of the men at the beginning and the end of the sentence*

	Werrington		Aylesbury	
	At the end	At the beginning Table II Chapter III	At the end	At the beginning Table II Chapter III
Food	2	8	—	23
Physical training and circuit training	4	21	2	5
Marching drill parades	1	14	4	9
Early rising and early P.T.	17	20	4	17
Changing	1	9	—	17
No smoking	4	10	7	13
Treatment by officers	—	12	4	4
Strictness of discipline	7	11	7	3
Lack of leisure, speed of programme	11	7	9	7
Scrubbing	—	7	—	11
Work	5	—	9	—
Being locked up	4	7	5	1

men, however, lost a great deal of their animosity to the whole process of physical training and some of them actually came to enjoy it. There was some reduction in the hardship suffered by the no-smoking rule and this is true of the Werrington and Aylesbury men alike. What remains is an increased or only slightly diminished dislike of those features of the centre which demanded the most continuous effort on the part of the inmates. The discipline, the general strictness of the regime, the lack of leisure and the speed of the day's programme, the amount of work rather than individual forms of it like scrubbing, all these remain as elements in the training which put pressure upon a considerable number of the men. Nevertheless, many of them had settled down to an acceptance of the routine that is reflected in the reduced number of complaints. One of the most intelligent of the men, who had been angry and resentful at his first interview summed up his own feelings and those of some of his fellows when he said, 'The whole place would be O.K. if it wasn't a gaol'.

This complaisance, however, is not necessarily a desirable aim for a penal institution. It has been argued[8] that if offenders have reached a stage in their detention at which they accept its rules and restrictions with equanimity, the whole value of the period of detention is lost. It is therefore pertinent to examine the general feeling with which this group looked back on their period of sentence. The answers to the question 'What have you felt most of the time here?' were not easy to tabulate since the men expressed themselves in very different ways. Some tabulation was, however, made possible by analysing the answers largely in accordance with specific words or phrases that occurred in them. For example, the word 'bored' might be used in conjunction with a more detailed description of the men's feelings. The following table shows the answers of the whole group to this general question.

Table 34: Answers to the question 'What have you felt most of the time here?'

	Werrington		Aylesbury		Total	
	No.	%	No.	%	No.	%
Miserable most of the time	20	36	9	20	29	29
Fairly happy	19	35	23	50	42	42
Bored, fed up	10	18	9	20	19	19
Angry, resentful	—	—	1	2	1	—
Others*	6	11	4	8	10	10
Total	55	100	46	100	101	100

* These include the men who said 'just existing', 'tensed up', 'frustrated' 'cross with himself for landing himself in this place' etc.

[8]Charles Meyer in *Journal of Criminal Law, Criminology and Police Science*, 1952, p. 155.

The answers of the men at their second interview are in fairly close accord with those that were given at the beginning of their sentence. Initially thirty-four men were miserable and homesick, fifteen were fairly happy, and thirty-two, although miserable at first, settled down to some measure of acceptance of their sentence. Thus the proportion of those who were continuously self-pitying, miserable or homesick is approximately the same at the beginning and the end of the period of detention. Any change that has occurred in the men's reaction to their sentence seems to be limited to a more ready acceptance of the frustrations, restrictions and difficulties that bore hard upon individual men.

One difference does, however, call for comment. Table 27 in Chapter III gives an analysis of the interviewer's assessment of the men's approach to the sentence imposed upon them. There it is shown that a degree of resentment that would be likely to impede the efficacy of the sentence was present in the attitude of sixteen men. At the end of the sentence this resentment had disappeared in all save one case. This is a man who professed disbelief in the efficacy of punishment of any sort. He said that all wrong-doing was caused by family difficulties and therefore punishment was useless. He said he was 'annoyed and aggrieved' most of the time he was at the centre. But his own background was disturbed and unhappy and he himself was difficult to handle, lacking any close friends and failing to attract the interest of the discipline staff at the centre.

Several items in the daily routine could be discussed only at the second interview. On these the men made many comments which could not be reduced to simple tabular form. Some thought that the evening activities were not sufficiently varied, some complained that the half-hour period of games, reading or talking was too short, particularly since the games provided, chess, draughts and so on, required a much longer time for their proper enjoyment. Others said that this period was too long—it was boring if there was nothing to do but read. This comment on the boredom of the leisure time that was available had particular reference to the week-end activities. There were no evening classes on Saturdays or Sundays, and, although there were games in the afternoons, some of the men felt that the evenings dragged along without point or stimulus.

The men's assessment of the worth of the evening classes which constituted the major activity on every week night could only be adequately made at the second interview. The classes provided at each centre were similar, English, arithmetic, woodwork, art and so on. The remarks made by some of the men were not very illuminating because they seemed to be at a loss to describe how they were helped or hindered by an evening activity which few of them had experienced since they left school. Nevertheless, the more articulate group at Aylesbury claimed that they had been helped in some way or another by some of the classes. Thirty-four men made comments that could be interpreted as favourable towards one class or another or as a general comment, nine of these made specific reference to the classes in current affairs. Several said the class was 'interesting', others said they 'learned a lot', they liked to hear other chaps talking. The art class was also found to be stimulating by some, but, because in Aylesbury at this time it was not possible for every man to choose his subject, some had to attend the art class four nights in the week, so that they became irritated and impatient. For the same reason, some of the men were quite unsuitable for the classes to which they were allotted. One very dull man remarked ruefully that he had 'got chokey[9] for sleeping in current affairs'. In examining the replies from the whole of the Aylesbury group it was found that seventeen men were bored or irritated by one or other of the classes which they themselves had attended.

When the men in the Werrington group made favourable comment on the classes, it was usually because they 'helped to pass the time' or because they 'got a good laugh'. There was little in the way of constructive comment. Twelve of the group had nothing to say of this part of the programme. The fullest comment came once more from one of the very dull men who said that in the current affairs class they 'talked about spacemen and nobody liked it very much'.

Relations of the men with staff at the centres

So far the analysis of the men's answers about the regimen of the centres has been concerned principally with tangible, perceptible things like meals, the routine of physical training, evening activities

[9]Chokey = detention in the cells.

and so on. Some consideration must now be given to the relationships within the centres, the attitude of the men to the officers and to each other. A tabulation of the replies to the question 'What do you think of the officers?' has been obtained by evaluating the comments and counting them as favourable, uncertain or hostile. The uncertain comments include all those who say 'some good, some bad', 'where they've been prison officers they're O.K., they're more worldly, borstal officers are not so good', and 'when they're all together they're awful, one by one O.K.', and 'the older ones are better' or contrariwise 'the younger ones are better, you can have a laugh with them'.

The following table shows all the final comments of the men on their reaction to the discipline staff and its task within the centre.

Table 35: Answers to the question 'What do you think of the officers?'
'Do you think the officers strict, severe, fair etc.?'

	Werrington		Aylesbury		Total No.
	No.	%	No.	%	
Favourable	37	67	9	20	46
Uncertain, not wholly favourable	15	28	34	73	49
Hostile	3	5	3	7	6
	55	100	46	100	101

'Do you think the officers strict, severe, fair etc.?'

	Werrington		Aylesbury		Total No.
	No.	%	No.	%	
Fair etc.	24	44	27	59	51
Mixed	13	23	10	21	23
Hostile	18	33	9	20	27
	55	100	46	100	101

At the first interview the men were asked for their reactions to the discipline staff in a slightly different way. The question was 'Do you find the officers . . . fair, strict, severe etc. and could you make friends with any of them? The answers to the first part of this question, which are given in Table 24, Chapter III for the whole group of 107 men, are, for convenience, reproduced here to show the responses of the 101 who spoke about the officers at the second interview also.

It would appear that, in the Werrington group the balance of feeling has swung over from hostility or doubt to approval, whereas the Aylesbury men at their second interview, showed considerably more hesitation about expressing unqualified appreciation of the officers as a whole. The reason for this change in attitude on the part of the Aylesbury men may lie in the phrasing of the questions themselves. At the second interview, when the men were simply asked 'What do you think of the officers?' all those who had any power of expression at all were able to dissect their feelings and express themselves in different ways with all the qualifications that personal preferences and experience of the centres demanded. This is probably why the answers of the Aylesbury group are more full of light and shade than the laconic answers of the men at Werrington where the percentage of those who express unqualified appreciation of the officers and their tasks has increased considerably.

At the second interview wholly unfavourable comments were rare. They include, however, such vicious remarks as 'They treat you like animals and expect you to treat them like gentlemen'. This man had received a number of minor and perhaps unofficial punishments such as extra scrubbing and had lost two days' remission for handing a piece of bread to another inmate while he was working in the kitchen. He was one of the few inmates visited by his probation officer during his sentence and he drew a comparison between probation officers and prison officers when he said 'prison officers told you to do something, probation officers only advised'. In the context this meant a severe condemnation of the officers. To the research worker who interviewed him this man appeared more mature and more reasonable than most but one of the prison officers had nothing good to say of him, his prospects were poor, his whole outlook was criminal and he had failed to benefit from his sentence of detention. It is probable that the hostile attitude of this man to all officers was due to the hostility which obviously existed between him and this single member of the discipline staff.

Several of the more independent men were aggrieved at having to address the officers as 'sir'. One wrote in a letter home that 'all the officers had been knighted'. The letter was stopped and retained in the man's file. A good deal of hostility was shown by this man both to his sentence and to the officers who were responsible for its execution, but in this case the reason was to be found in the mental disturbance which had been apparent in him since his early childhood. The officers reporting on him did not expect him to keep out of further trouble, but his obvious resentment was put down to bewilderment by one officer and the general tone of the reports upon him suggested that his hostility was understood. Such a relationship of kindliness and understanding that sometimes existed between men and officers was particularly well illustrated in the case of men of low intelligence. There were at the centres several of these dull, helpless, almost illiterate men. At the beginning of their period of detention the interviewers found that these men had difficulty in understanding and answering the questions that were put to them. When they were seen for a second time there was a change in their appearance and their attitude. They were smarter, more articulate in speech and they gave the appearance of being fairly happy. The officers did not always realize the extent of the men's disabilities[10] but they were sympathetic and kindly to men who seemed genuinely unable to cope with the difficulties of the centre. The men responded by making as much effort as they could. This improvement in behaviour did not always persist beyond the period of detention. Two of these dull men were reconvicted a short time after their release.

Other evidence of the relationship between men and officers is to be found in the punishments which the men incurred in the course of their sentence, since the incidence of punishment is an index not only of the response of the men to their training but also of the reaction of the discipline staff to the results of their measures of discipline.

The principal forms of punishment, forfeiture of remission and detention in the detention cells were accurately reported by the men and could be checked against the report forms in the files. The following table shows the incidence of these two major forms

[10]The officers did not remark upon the low intelligence of these men when they were asked to assess their ability and comprehension.

of punishment at the two centres. Although the figures are small it is clear that, in relation to the group that is being studied, loss of remission was used more frequently than detention as a serious form of punishment both at Werrington and at Aylesbury.

Table 36: Punishments awarded to the men at Werrington and Aylesbury

	Werrington		Aylesbury		Total No.
	No.	%	No.	%	
Loss of remission	13	27	22	47	35
Detention in cells	11	20	5	11	16
	24	47	27	58	51

The behaviour of the Aylesbury group and the response of the officers to this behaviour seemed to be worse than that of the men at Werrington.[11] The misdeeds for which these punishments were given emphasizes the difference between the centres. Smoking, which was regarded as a serious offence in view of the strict rule against it, was discovered and punished eleven times at Aylesbury and twice at Werrington. The opportunities for breaking this rule were, of course, more numerous at Aylesbury and some of the men described in great detail how cigarettes could be smuggled in when the centre was in course of construction and the staff was small. Absconding, which is the gravest of all crimes in the context of any institutional treatment, occurred twice at Aylesbury and once at Werrington during the whole course of the research. In each case it was punished by loss of remission. The smuggling out of letters was also said to be easy, and although there is no evidence how often this was successful, six men out of the research group were caught and punished for this offence at Aylesbury and no one at Werrington. The possession of unauthorized articles or

[11]The men at Aylesbury were almost unanimous in their account of the discipline at the centre for some time after it was opened. The officers told them that they were 'having it easy' and it would be much more difficult for those who came in later. Perhaps because they were conscious of this freedom, the men misbehaved more often and punishments were given to remind them that rules did exist although it was not always easy to enforce them.

the attempt to obtain or distribute them fell within the offences thought to be sufficiently serious to merit loss of remission. At Aylesbury, one man passed on bread to another, a second was found to be in possession of two towels and a third stole margarine from the kitchen for his hair.[12]

The disciplinary punishments imposed at Werrington were for less well-defined offences, for horseplay, for fighting, for tattooing, for 'making a noise like a cat and making everyone laugh', and so on.

Men were sent to the cells for offences that were slightly less serious, 'going to sleep in current affairs', 'laughing at the cook', saying a rude word to the art teacher and other misdemeanours of this kind. There were also minor punishments such as extra duties, loss of earnings, early rising and even early bed. This last was given to one man who had been sent to clean the chapel unsupervised. He fell asleep and was punished by having to go to bed early for a week. Accurate details of these minor punishments are not easy to obtain but according to the accounts of the men there were twenty-five such minor awards at Werrington and forty-three at Aylesbury.

On this evidence of the punishments which were given and the offences which earned them, it appears that the Aylesbury group was, in the eyes of the discipline staff at least, more unruly and less ready to accept their sentence than the men at Werrington. This fact may be the cause or the effect of the men's attitude to the officers themselves. Table 35 on p. 106 shows that the Aylesbury group had many more doubts about the officers than the simpler Werrington men.[13]

Several other factors were considered that might distinguish those who were punished from those who were not, age, assess-

[12]An amusing sidelight on the abuse of punishment was the case of a man at Aylesbury who wanted to lose two days' remission in order to go out on the same day as a friend of his. He engineered this quite successfully by spilling paint on the floor of the art class, earning a report from the art master and then receiving his two days forfeiture of remission from the Warden.

[13]The Report of the Prison Commissioners for 1961 shows (Table A6) that the disciplinary punishments awarded to the men at Werrington were lower than at any other detention centre, junior or senior. (1.6 was the annual number of offences per head of the average population. The figure for Aylesbury was 2 2).

ment of criminality by the officers, and so on, but no clear pattern of relationship emerged with the following exceptions : eleven out of the twenty men whose sentences were longer than three months were included in the number of men who forfeited some part of their remission. It is true that the period of risk for six-month and four-month men was greater than for all the others, but the more convincing reason for this proportionate strength of the longer-sentence offenders in the figure for severe punishment is that the deterrent effect of loss of remission was not so great for those who had longer to serve. They were not able to envisage the end of their sentence and carelessness or rebellion would provoke the kind of action which resulted in punishment. Oddly too, there was a proportionately large number of violent offenders in the group that received punishment of this kind, seven of the total of eighteen violent offenders lost some part of their remission, and other disciplinary punishments were frequently incurred.

Detention centres do not claim to provide specific incentives to good behaviour save by the awarding of grades for good work and obedience to the rules of the centre. All the men at Werrington and Aylesbury entered upon grade I when their sentence began. Promotion to grade II followed, generally in about four weeks, but failure to attain this grade after a certain length of time was punished by loss of remission. This was only done in a few cases in the whole group. During the course of this research, grade III was awarded only at the established centre at Werrington. There, twenty-seven out of the fifty-five men whose behaviour and attitudes were studied both at the beginning and the end of their sentence were promoted to this highest grade. This was the group whom the officers thought were serving their sentence as they should. Among them there were few whom the officers regarded as criminal in a real sense, few who regarded themselves as criminal. In general their prospects were regarded as being good both by the officers and themselves. In age they were in no way different from the whole group, nor in the offence for which they had been committed to the centres. They included some of the very dull men, and two whose brusqueness of manner was probably derived from their experience of fairs and fairgrounds. These two, however, were capable of hard work and may have recommended themselves to the officers on this account.

Relation between the inmates

The impact on the detention centre inmates of the discipline staff is probably less powerful than the influence of the whole group upon each of its members. Some of the men were committed to the centre with those who were convicted with them, others found there men from their own neighbourhood with whom they could share experiences. The remainder took their place in this new community as best they could. The majority settled down well and made their detention tolerable by finding acceptance among those who were also there. A few remained aloof throughout the sentence. Table 37 shows the answers of the whole group to the question 'Have you made any friends at the centre?'

In most cases the men indicated the extent of this friendliness by saying they would meet or write to the friends they had made. Often this is no more than a gesture which may never be carried out but it shows the frame of mind in which they face their re-settlement. Only nine in the whole group said they did not make any special friends. This is more true of the Werrington men, six of whom did not seem to have been well received in the community of the centre. One of these, a very unstable young man who was convicted on several occasions of indecent exposure, complained that the other men 'picked on him'.[14] The man convicted of rape was also unpopular and said that he had made no friends.

Table 37:

	Werrington	Aylesbury	Total
Have made friends and will or may meet	27	33	60
Will write	3	1	4
No mention of meeting or may not meet	16	9	25
Have not made any special friends	6	3	9
No adequate answer	3	—	3
	55	46	101

In each of these cases the reason was probably to be found in the personality of the offenders rather than the nature of the offence of which they were known to have been convicted. Neither

[14]This was the only man in the whole sample whose unpopularity was agreed upon by more than one of the officers reporting on him.

of them was at all attractive in character or in person. Another young man, also at Werrington, who was himself markedly more intelligent than most of the others said 'some of the lads are dead thick'. For this reason he could find, as he thought, no adequate companionship. At Werrington there seemed to be a deliberate policy on the part of the staff to discourage alliances that might lead to trouble outside. The Aylesbury group were more ready and more able to resist attempts to destroy the detention centre community. It has been noted already that they were a more homogeneous group of sophisticated young men. Three only rejected the others and were rejected by them. A dull and unattractive first offender was deeply ashamed of his offence and resolved to have no part in its consequences. Another young man, intelligent but slick and insincere, made no friends, probably because he was found to be too clever and calculating. By and large, however, the men were friendly and sympathetic to one another. There were some natural leaders in the group whose names recurred quite often in the discussions with the men. At first the interviewers thought these might be men with six months sentences whose experience gave them some sort of hold over the others. This does not appear to be wholly true, for men with longer sentences than the normal three months sometimes complained that their friends were all discharged before them so that the latter part of their sentence was boring and isolated.[15] In Werrington the name of a certain individual was repeatedly mentioned by the new inmates. Although he did not fall within the limits of the sample, he was seen and agreed to answer the questions that were being addressed to the others. He was in fact, serving a six-months' sentence, but he was also older than most of the men, being nearly twenty-one, and he gave the impression of being mature and sober, but the officers reporting on this man agreed in their assessments upon him. He was criminal in outlook, and his prospects were poor. Yet he was popular among the men and his influence was considerable.

The opportunities for exchanging views or making friendly contacts are reduced to a minimum by the strict regimen of the centres. Nevertheless, during the evening period of 'association' half an hour before supper, the men may read, play games or talk

[15]The officers felt that men with longer sentences were more popular than some of the others. See Chapter V, p. 90.

freely. They also talk at meal times when they are seated four at a table. During working hours there is not much opportunity for free discussion, but some men, nearing the end of their sentence, work in relative freedom from supervision. The interchange of ideas at this point when the men have come to some conclusion about their offences and sentence, must be important but the extent and nature of this interchange is difficult to measure. Generally, the men say they talk about what happens during the day, about when they are going out and what they will do then. It has been possible to list also the majority of other topics which the men say are discussed among them. Each subject is given a single mark, but each man may be counted two or three times by giving more than one answer.

Table 38 : Answers to the question 'What do you talk about ?'

	Werrington	Aylesbury	Total
Happenings of the day	26	26	52
Date of release and plans for release	23	18	41
Girls and girl-friends	11	11	22
What happens at home and what the men have done outside	7	5	12
Drink	6	5	11
Cigarettes	3	6	9

There were several snap answers that may have been learned off to impress the interviewers or that have been current as jocular expressions when the men were airing their grievances among themselves. One of these was that they talked of 'beer, women and cigarettes'. That this was a phrase accepted as symbolic of all that men were thinking about was evidenced by the fact that the dullest man in the whole group who was quite incapable of original thought and was, besides, almost inarticulate gave this ready answer when he was asked what he talked about in the centre. Another stereotyped reply was 'screwing'.[16] This was used to indicate that they were accustomed to talk of their exploits outside the centre. Talk of drinking and cigarettes shows that some of the men took these deprivations seriously but the majority seem to be absorbed with the events of each day or the expectation of release.

[16]thieving.

But the importance of the men's relationship with each other cannot be measured simply by their own account of their conversations with their fellows. It was reflected also in the language the men used in their discussions with the interviewers, in the more obvious changes that had taken place in their attitudes and in their evaluation of the kind of community in which they had been living for the last months.

The self-conscious use of a recently learned jargon gave evidence of the willingness with which some men identified themselves with the more criminal elements at each centre, although it is possible that this may be due to a naïveté that responded to the piquancy of a new language. One young man whose career outside was not criminal in the accepted sense, since his offences were principally violations of the Road Traffic Acts, was careful to show how much he knew of crime by punctuating his remarks with references to arrests for 'suss' to 'grassing', 'screwing' and so on.[17] This man was married and his wife was expecting a child; nevertheless some part of his converse with his fellows at the centre was devoted to arranging a motor-cycle spree to Blackpool about the time when his child would be born.

A change of attitude that was puzzling to the interviewer occurred in another man of a different type. He too was a traffic offender (driving while disqualified) with only one previous offence of carrying an unqualified passenger on his motor-cycle. He was angry at being sent to the centre because his family circumstances were difficult and his earnings were needed at home. Later, though he accepted the routine at the centre and did well, he rejected entirely its power to prevent the repetition of offences and said that nothing could stop law-breaking for it was due to the district a man lived and the upbringing he had. Then came a surprising outburst of racial feeling. Among other things he said 'a lot of darkies lead to trouble, a lot of people are against darkies'. He admitted that he was too. There was no sign of this attitude at the first interview,

[17]'suss' = a charge of being a suspected person. Power of arrest is given to a constable in the case of persons loitering at night in a highway or yard whom he reasonably suspects of having committed or even of being about to commit a felony. In London a constable has even wider powers.
'grassing' = giving information to police, prison officers or others in authority.
'screwing = thieving.

no sign of the general truculence that was now apparent and it is possible to conclude that views of this kind were due to talk among the men (two of whom had been sent to the centre for their part in a racial affray). Another evidence of the deterioration in his attitude was the remark that he did not regret his offences at all, only the consequences of them. This may reflect a conviction fairly generally held in the detention centre and outside that traffic offences are not at all criminal nor are they punishable in the same way as crimes. This offender's definition of a criminal was 'a murderer and a wife-beater' so that he could not regard either himself or any of his fellows as criminals. This new morality might be attributed to discussions with other men at the centre, since earlier conversations with him had not revealed any hint of it.

Apart from these examples of the attitudes that the men communicate to each other, some measure of their awareness of criminality can be obtained by examining their answer to the question 'What is a criminal?' The answers to this question are roughly tabulated below, showing the normal distinction between Werring-

Table 39: Answers to the question 'What is a criminal?'

	Werrington	Aylesbury	Total
Persistent offenders	18	16	34
Those found guilty of robbery	14	7	21
Those found guilty of theft	11	6	17
Those found guilty of violence	8	6	14
Those found guilty of murder	5	2	7
Those found guilty of taking and driving cars	1	—	1
One who is in prison and over 21	—	1	1
One who is in prison	2	2	4
Those who do not abide by the law	3	5	8
Misfits	1	—	1
Shopkeepers	—	1	1

ton and Aylesbury. Such other distinctions as might be expected to appear, seem to have been obliterated by the consciousness of community among the men. The offences for which they were committed are not remembered as important, except in the case of rape, perhaps of indecent exposure and one or two of the traffic offenders.

Several men said they did not know who was a criminal, in some cases two definitions were given and these are counted separately in the table. The man who defined criminals as shopkeepers was a clever, maladjusted, bitter young man who had a long history of difficult and delinquent conduct and of treatment in special schools for maladjusted children. He blamed his own misdeeds on an evil world so that his definition of criminality was quite consistent with his philosophy. The largest proportion of the men define crime in terms of serious and violent transgressions of the law. By implication, therefore, there are no criminals in the centres. Even the one man who was charged with conspiracy to rob, denied that he was a criminal for they were 'chaps who plan quite big robberies and those that go round murdering'.

It is quite clear, however, that the men do not really relate their conception of crime in general to the fact of their own offences. Only fifteen men out of the whole group of 101 were willing to admit that they should be classed as criminals. These were offenders of all kinds, thieves, violent offenders, one committed for non-payment of a fine and another for carrying an offensive weapon, three offenders found guilty of taking and driving, and one convicted of receiving. The question 'Are there any criminals here?' was not asked in every case. It was introduced only at a later stage of the project because experience had shown it to be helpful. Of the seventy-seven men who were asked this question forty-eight said that the centres contained some criminals, twenty-nine said they did not.

As a natural consequence of this evidence on the men's attitude to the criminality of themselves and their fellows at the centres, it is pertinent to consider whether they thought they were sent to the right place. The following table shows the answers to the question 'Do you think you were sent to the right place?' with comparative answers to the question 'Was this the right punishment?' which was asked at the first interview.

At the beginning of their sentence more than half of the men were not prepared to accept the sentence. Although the interviewers felt that there was a real difference in the attitude of the men at the end of their sentence, some weight must be given to the fact that the question at the second interview was framed in a slightly different way from the parallel question put to the men at the beginning of their sentence. At that early point the question

117

was 'Do you think this was the right punishment for your offence?' The men were therefore asked to consider their sentence in relation to all the other measures available to the court which sentenced them. The question was framed the second time to focus attention on the institutional nature of the sentence. The men were asked whether they thought they had been sent to the right place.

Table 40:

	Werrington				Aylesbury			
	Sent to the right place Interview II		Right punishment Interview I		Sent to the right place Interview II		Right punishment Interview I	
	No.	%	No.	%	No.	%	No.	%
Yes	38	70	19	32	23	51	21	44
No.	10	16	31	53	16	36	24	50
Uncertain	7	14	9	15	7	13	3	6
	55	100	59	100	46	100	48	100

It is therefore possible that some of the men interpreted the question in this strict sense and gave their answers accordingly. Consideration of the negative answers to the question put during the second interview gives some indication of what the men really meant. Four of the ten negative answers of the Werrington group came from first offenders, the others were given by men who did not think they were guilty of the offences as charged or from men who thought they had been provoked or who thought their offence and record did not deserve institutional treatment. Of the Aylesbury men who said that they had not been sent to the right place, one denied the offence, four were first offenders, two thought they should have had prison and one expected borstal. The others thought they should not have been sent away at all. In a few cases detention was not thought to be effective.

A useful footnote to the assessment of the value and correctness of the sentence given in this last answer is to be found in the replies to the question 'What sentence would you give to an offender like yourself with your own offence and record?' In general the men knew little of the use of different forms of punishment. They were alive to the fact that first offenders should be lightly, if not generously treated, and in considering the punishment of hypothetical offenders, their first question was 'Was this a first offence?' Beyond this and a rather crude belief in the value of prison as a deterrent, they were not able to go. In regard to their own offence they had firm views and thirty-six of them said they would give themselves a sentence other than the one they had received. Table 41 shows the numbers of those who would accept a detention sentence of any length and those who would prefer or thought they deserved a different form of treatment.

Table 41 : Answers to the question 'What sentence would you give for your own offence and record ?'

	Werrington	Aylesbury	Total
Detention sentence of any length	28	24	52
Prison	1	4	5
Borstal	2	2	4
Probation	2	8	10
Fine	11	4	15
Conditional discharge	1	1	2
No punishment	2	1	3
No clear answer	8	2	10
	55	46	101

Some of the men (10) rejected detention for themselves because they thought that, as first offenders, they had a right to leniency, others denied the offences of which they were found guilty. Others would have preferred different treatment. There was no evidence that the nature of the offence was connected in any way with the offender's attitude to his sentence now that it was nearly over. Such differences as do exist are related rather to the ecological group to which the offenders belong. On the whole the Werrington men were more prepared to accept such lessons as the centre had to offer, less inclined to question their sentence. Nevertheless, on the evidence available, it is clear that slightly more than half of the whole group of offenders accepted their sentence in retrospect and bore no grudge against the process of the law as they prepared to return to normal conditions of life.

Where the men did accept the sentence as effective and right, the reason for this acceptance is not readily apparent in what the men thought they were being taught at the centre or in what they had learned. The answers to the first of these two questions had been tabulated so as to compare with the figures given in Table 26 of Chapter III where the answers to a similar question are set out.

Table 42: Answers to the question 'Do you think you have learned anything?'

	Werrington		Aylesbury		Total	
	End of sentence	Begin-ning of sentence	End of sentence	Begin-ning of sentence	End of sentence	Begin-ning of sentence
Deterrent lesson	22	13	17	13	39	26
Discipline	16	15	18	9	34	24
Physical fitness	2	4	1	2	3	6
Work habits	1	1	1	5	2	6
Other things	13	4	—	4	13	8
Nothing	12	26	18	15	30	41

It is clear from these figures that the conception of the sentence as being utterly valueless has become less strong—instead it is regarded by nearly four out of every ten men as teaching the lesson that they must not offend again. The table, compressed in this way, cannot do justice to the variety and sometimes the thoughtfulness of the answers that were given.

Speaking of what they had themselves learned, some gave examples of the actual physical accomplishments they had acquired. They had learned to march and to do physical training, to read and write and to work hard. Whether they had been taught a deeper lesson seemed to be worrying some of the men. A thoughtful northerner, who had not a great reputation for intelligence but appeared to be mature and independent remarked that he had learned farm work but he was just the same person inside. He implied in all that he said that the detention centre had failed in its object since the officers were trying to make the men different by discipline and routine. Another man said that he supposed he hadn't learned anything because he had been told so by the officers. A few said they had learned not to get caught. One

offender found guilty of violence had, at first, been truculent, unco-
operative and difficult. Seen for a second time he was much more
co-operative, slick in his answers and almost knowing. He said he
had learned 'not to be so moody'. Nevertheless it was of this man
that the officers said he was a 'younger version of what could be
seen in Dartmoor'. A humorous evaluation of the value of different
parts of the sentence was given by another of the violent offenders
who had been found guilty of assaulting a policeman. He also
began his training in a mood of rebellion but later began to enjoy
himself, and became the comedian of the centre. In answer to
the question 'What had he learned?', he replied 'Crime doesn't
pay and how to use a scrubbing brush'.[18]

Possibility of further offences

Having considered the centres in all their aspects from their
restrictions to their positive teaching the men were directed to
turn their attention to their own future conduct after their release.

It would be natural to expect that any group of offenders looking forward to their discharge from a penal institution would
reply to the question 'Do you think you will get into trouble again?'
with a firm negative. This was not in fact the case, and,
although only one man said that he would probably be in trouble
within a few months, seventeen expressed doubts about their
capacity to avoid further offences. Three men at Werrington
thought they would be safe if they didn't drink. Two others at the
same centre thought they might be provoked into violence. (One
of these men had a violent temper and said that he would get into
trouble 'if someone hit him very hard'.) Another of the Werrington
group who had done exceedingly well at the centre and seemed
at the first interview not at all delinquent in outlook, said
he wouldn't get into trouble because he wouldn't risk being
caught. But implicit in this and in the general tone of this part of
the discussion with him, was the thought that he might risk something if the chances of being caught were negligible. An offender
found guilty of driving while disqualified said he would only
commit motoring offences. At Aylesbury the men were less sure

[18]This man, however, who had been a miner since leaving school, left
this job when he left the centre and found a less well-paid employment as
a bricklayer. See Chapter VII, p. 126.

of their reasons for possible recidivism. One said 'he didn't know, he would wait and see', another said he wouldn't offend unless the cost was less than the gain,[19] and another, 'if it was something worth while and for a lot of money' he would offend again. The remarks of the officers who warned some of the men that they would soon be 'inside' again increased the uncertainty with which this small group faced the outcome of detention. One man in particular had been told by the officers that he would be 'inside again within three months'. He was very anxious about this and repeatedly asked for assurances that this would not be so. Information reaching the centre shortly after his release showed that he had been before the court for some minor offence and was bound over. But he had been held in custody on remand, so that technically at least he had been 'inside' within three months. This assessment of their future prospects does not match the men's statements about their own criminality. Of the fifteen who admitted they were to be regarded as criminals only five were uncertain about their capacity to keep out of trouble.

Nevertheless, although the final outcome of the punishment of these men is not fully known, there is evidence to suggest that the regimen of the centres had affected some change in the attitude of the men. They were less resentful, more appreciative of the task of the staff, more ready to agree that they had been taught a lesson at the centre and that the centre had some purpose. What is more difficult to assess is the development of the relation between the men themselves and any changes that might take place, as a result of this, in their acceptance of social duties and responsibilities.

So far, the men whose attitudes and adjustment were being examined had answered questions related to matters within their own experience, and, in particular, to the offences they had committed and their legal consequences. At the end of the second interview certain general questions were added, some of which at least, had reference to matters on which the men could express general opinions only, based not on their own personal knowledge, but on views and sentiments which they would acquire from their

[19]This man expressed in colloquial Cockney exactly what Beccaria said of the quantum of punishment: 'It is sufficient that the evil it occasions should exceed the good expected from the crime, including in the calculation the certainty of punishment and the privation of the expected advantage.'

own group, or would assimilate as members of the wider community in which they lived.

It was hoped by this means and by individual case studies to provide a general picture of the men considered apart from their experience of the detention centres. Few, however, were able to give clear answers to questions which asked for opinions on matters beyond the frontier of their own experience. The answers recorded here, therefore, provide only a few indications of the ideas which form the background to the daily lives of men who have been punished for criminal behaviour.

They were asked, for example to suggest measures which might stop young men from getting into trouble so frequently. To this the answers were as numerous and diverse as the men themselves. Some agreed on the need for early discipline and training (the interest and co-operation of fathers was thought to be particularly necessary here), some would have more youth clubs and active interests for young men. One man said that no one would stop committing crimes until he had been caught, another declared that nothing would stop thieving but violent offences might be stopped by violent punishment.

On the subject of corporal punishment opinion was evenly divided between those who thought it would deter and those who did not. In the matter of their own preference for violent punishment as opposed to detention, they had little to guide them, since they had no idea what corporal punishment involved. The father of one man, who had witnessed a flogging in the navy, described the process to his son and remarked that it was useful in preventing crime. The men themselves had two criteria: the time taken to administer a punishment, and in this corporal punishment was preferable to detention, and the possibility of lasting effects, and here the physical disfigurement resulting from physical punishment was thought by some to be more frightening than detention.

The theory of punishment that was implicit in the hypothetical sentences the men gave to hypothetical offenders[20] is one of retri-

[20]The question asked was: Imagine yourself a judge. Sentence the following people.
(1) Someone who coshes and robs a shopkeeper
(2) Someone who breaks and enters
(3) Someone who repeatedly steals small things
(4) Someone with your own record and present offence

bution. The punishment should fit the crime, or series of crimes in which the criminal has been detected and imprisonment was regarded as the just due of serious offenders or the recidivist, not necessarily because it would do any good but because it would satisfy the demands of fairplay as between the community and the offender. Only one man expressed any regard for the actual victim of crime. He thought that punishment should involve compensation to the victim of crime for loss or injury suffered.

The men's response to a fourth general question 'What is your opinion of the police?' was based upon knowledge and experience, however limited, so that the answers, although varied, were more specific and more forceful than the first three. Slightly more than half of the group were prepared to admit that the police had a job to do and, within limits, they did it reasonably well. One or two of the violent offenders who maintained that they had been roughly handled by the police, were still resentful, but one of the most vehement of these, who had spent a disproportionate part of his first interview inveighing against the police, calling them 'sadists' and 'criminals', had modified his view and now said that they were 'unfair—especially in the city'. Other men expressed particular dislike of young policemen, saying that they were 'big-headed' or of all policemen because they were 'against teenagers', they were 'unjust legally' and so on. Some of the group that disliked the police feared that when they went out, they would be 'picked on' and brought before the courts again simply because they had been 'inside'.

It may be true that the period of detention had modified the attitude of these men towards the police and the processes of the law. They were agreed that the execution of the sentence of detention had not been unbearable but they would not like to repeat it. They were resolved not to get into trouble again if only because the consequence would be a further loss of liberty, but whether they were able to maintain this resolve after their release, whether their conduct was any better than it was before the experience of detention is a different matter. The following chapter sets out what is known about this group of offenders in the six months following their release.

CHAPTER SIX

A LIMITED FOLLOW-UP OF THESE
YOUNG MEN AFTER THEIR DISCHARGE

BECAUSE of the limitations of time and resources, the plan
of this research did not provide for a full follow-up of the group
whose attitudes and adjustments were studied within the centres.
Some information about what happened to them was, however,
obtained from the replies to a questionnaire sent to each man
about four months after his discharge. Although, when they were
asked if they would fill in and return this form, all the men agreed
to co-operate, only thirty-seven out of 101 did in fact do so. In
eight other cases (four from each centre) the enquiry form was
returned by the postal authorities because the man could not be
traced. Thus fifty-six out of the ninety-three (60 per cent.) who
could be presumed to have received the enquiry form did not
return it. Yet the questionnaire was simple. It asked for details
of the man's employment, of his adjustment to family and friends
and his plans for the future. The questions could be answered by
marking certain items so that actual writing could be avoided.
Stamped and addressed envelopes were provided so that failure
to comply with the request for information could only be due
to indifference or hostility.

From the point of view of the research workers this was a dis-
appointing result, since no firm conclusions could be based on
information that covered less than 40 per cent. of the whole
sample. It was, however, no part of the research plan to pursue
these young men so as to elicit an answer from them. After the
form had been sent out once, it was not re-issued, nor was
any special effort made to obtain a reply.

Twenty-five out of the thirty-seven men who sent back the
enquiry form said that they had remained at home and had en-

countered no difficulties there. The remainder had either left home or faced such difficulties with their families that they contemplated doing so. Such a break was seldom the result of the detention centre sentence since most of these men had been at loggerheads with their immediate circle even before their committal. Indeed some of them may have remained at home too long before their detention and returned to it too readily after their discharge. Nevertheless their departure following so close upon a sentence of detention which must have increased their domestic difficulties might reduce the chance of a proper adjustment to a life away from home.

Consideration of the employment history of the men after their discharge may provide stronger evidence of their social adjustment. The period covered by this part of the enquiry, from release until the return of the questionnaire, was four or at the most five months, so that the men were able to give a clear answer to the question about the number of jobs they had had in this time, although the reasons for change of job or unemployment are not always clear.

Before the sentence of detention it was obvious that many of the men were unemployed by their own choice. After discharge, however, most of those who answered the enquiry seem to have made an effort to obtain and hold a job. Yet the answers to the enquiry indicate that a few at least would prefer to be unemployed than to have jobs that they considered pointless or that they did not like. It is possible that, because they had served a sentence of detention, they were offered jobs that no one else would take, but there is also evidence that those who were unemployed after their discharge had an unsatisfactory record before they were sentenced.

Slightly more than half (nineteen out of thirty-six) changed their jobs once or twice since their release and included in this number were ten men whose record before their sentence of detention was reasonably good. One disturbing example of this restlessness was quite unexpected. a rough, tough Midlander who had been working as a coalminer, and who said, during his detention that he would not wish to do anything else (the pay was good) had three jobs since his release from detention and ended up with a wage considerably lower than he was used to in mining. He was the sole support of his family and this drop in income must have been of considerable consequence to them.

The restlessness in employment shown by some of the group of thirty-seven men is aggravated by other difficulties which were described in detail by those who took the trouble to give a verbal account of their post-release history. Ten men expressed in writing their appreciation or their criticism of their sentence and its results, or else they explained their present difficulties. In addition the mothers of two men wrote, one thanking the authorities for all that had been done for her son, the other seeking help in her son's employment difficulties. The men themselves were generally critical. There were complaints about their treatment at the labour exchanges, they were not given any assistance in finding jobs and generally they had to find them for themselves. One man said he had been seriously hampered by a long period of driving disqualification. He was a steeplejack and could not travel as far as he might because he was not able to drive the firm's van. His general comment was that he had 'paid' for his misdeeds by a sentence of detention, why should he be disqualified as well? Another wrote a bald statement of fact; in the four months since his discharge he had had a 'nervous breakdown' and spent six weeks in hospital. The two most intelligent men in the group wrote comments on the sentence itself. One said 'I think it would be better to sentence people to one month's detention, because after that it just becomes a way of life and it doesn't teach you a lesson.'[1] The other wrote 'I don't think detention is any good—it was just an experience like going up in an aeroplane for the first time. What it will be like the next time, I don't know.' It is significant that both these men were reconvicted, but after the six-months' follow-up so that they are not included as reconvictions in the study which follows. One is now in borstal and the other on probation.

In addition to the information obtained from these questionnaires, details of further court appearances were obtained from the centres, each of which is notified of any subsequent conviction of the men who had served a sentence of detention there.

[1]This man, of considerable intelligence seemed to be reacting against his family's social aspirations. His sister had obtained a good secretarial job and since she spent her vacations at home, attempted to share her social and educational advancement with her family. The man himself was attending night classes but these were interrupted by his sentence and he said he would not return to them. He expressed scorn of his sister's acquisition of a new voice and attitude.

Within a period of six months after the discharge of each of the men in the group, eighteen notifications of further convictions had been received. Of these, three concerned offences which had been committed before the sentence of detention. One of these men was committed to borstal, one was put on probation and the third was fined. These three are excluded from the consideration of the reconvictions which follows. The remaining fifteen, each of whom was reconvicted within so short a period of discharge, could be considered as the most significant failures of the whole group of 101 men. By the same token, those who showed sufficient sense of responsibility and interest to answer the questionnaire and who were themselves not reconvicted, could be considered as the most successful. Thus, the thirty-seven men who answered the questionnaire has been reduced to thirty-four to exclude the three who were also reconvicted within the specified period. Comparing these two groups, those who were reconvicted and those who answered the questionnaire, it is possible to detect certain similarities and differences which might suggest a basis for further and fuller enquiry at some other time.

With all the reservations which such small numbers must dictate, it would appear that in the reconvicted group there is an appreciably larger proportion of dishonest offenders and a smaller proportion of violent offenders than in the group which answered the questionnaire and in the sample group as a whole.[2] This result is largely due to the small number of dishonest offenders among the Werrington men. In the Aylesbury group there was little difference in the proportion of dishonest offenders who were reconvicted and those who were not.

The previous proved offences of the men in these two groups indicate a further difference between them for those who were reconvicted include a disproportionate number of men with four and more than four previous offences. (Table 43).

[2]This finding is confirmed by other evidence of the dishonesty of the failure group. Every one of the fifteen men who were reconvicted within the prescribed period had, at some period in his criminal history, been found guilty of an offence of dishonesty. In the group which answered the questionnaire seven out of thirty-four (20 per cent.) were free of any conviction for a dishonest offence.

*Table 43: Table showing previous proved offences of those who answered the
questionnaire and those who were reconvicted*

	34 men answering		Both	15 men reconvicted		Both
	Werrington	Aylesbury		Werrington	Aylesbury	
No previous offences	3	3	6	1	2	3
1–3 previous offences	9	13	22	2	1	3
4+ previous offences	3	3	6	5	4	9
Total	15	19	34	8	7	15

The previous sentences of the two groups have been considered
but no clear differences emerged that were not already disclosed
by the examination of the previous proved offences.

When other factors besides the criminal experience of the two
groups are considered, there are still differences between them.
For example, those who have been reconvicted are younger than
the parallel group of thirty-four men not reconvicted, and proportionately younger than the whole group. (Table 44).

Table 44: Age grouping of 34 men not re-convicted and 15 men reconvicted

Age at sentence to detention	34 not reconvicted			15 reconvicted		
	Werring-ton	Ayles-bury	Both	Werring-ton	Ayles-bury	Both
Aged 17	4	7	11(32%)	5	4	9(60%)
Aged 18	5	6	11(32%)	—	2	2(13%)
Aged 19	3	5	8(24%)	2	1	3(20%)
Aged 20	3	1	4(12%)	1	—	1(7%)
Total	15	19	34	8	7	15

In their record of employment before committal to detention,
the reconvicted men are seen to have a slightly higher proportion
of job changes than the corresponding group of those who were

not reconvicted. The employment record of the whole group of 107 men who formed the basis of the original enquiry is shown in Chapter II. The majority (65 per cent.) had a record of more than one year as the longest time, in any one employment. This figure comes close to the proportion (70 per cent.) for men with a stable record of employment in the group of thirty-four men who were not reconvicted. Those who were reconvicted were fairly evenly divided among those who kept their jobs and those who did not.

Table 45: Longest period spent in any one employment before the sentence of detention

Longest period in one job	34 men not reconvicted			15 men reconvicted		
	Werrington	Aylesbury	Both	Werrington	Aylesbury	Both
1 year or more	12	11	23	4	4	8
Less than 1 year	3	7	10	4	3	7
Not known	—	1	1	—	—	—
Total	15	19	34	8	7	15

In those factors which are connected with the men's environment and previous history, their employment, their record of criminality and their most recent offence, there is some measure of difference between those who were reconvicted and those who were not. There is slighter evidence of any connection between length of sentence and reconviction. Out of twenty men in the sample with sentences of more than three months, four people were reconvicted within four months of their release. So too, in the officers' reports on the men's progress in training and in their general behaviour within the centre, there is nothing to distinguish those who offend again from those who do not. The officers did, however, make some adverse comment on the criminality of the individuals in the group that was reconvicted. This is possibly because they were aware of the previous criminal history of this group and it has been shown that a high proportion had previous offences recorded against them.

At an early stage of the study (Chapter III) an attempt was made to measure and record the research workers' assessments of the attitude of the men towards their training. When this assessment is matched with the reconvictions and the response to the questionnaire of the present group of forty-nine men there is evidence that both in the reconvicted and the non-reconvicted group there are fewer than average men with 'satisfactory' attitudes. This is perhaps to be expected with the 'failure' group, it was more surprising to find it a feature of the small group which took the trouble to answer the questionnaire. The explanation may be that, whereas the 'failure' group contained a higher proportion of 'light-hearted' or 'cocksure' men, those who answered the questionnaire were more often 'miserable and depressed'. This depression may have been the very factor which caused the men to answer the questionnaire.

Although the comparison of the men who were reconvicted with those who were not was limited to a period of six months after release, information was also available about seven other men who reappeared before the courts more than six months after they were discharged. Three were sent to borstal, two put on probation and two fined.

Thus, before the research project was finally completed twelve men were confined in some form of institution. One was in a mental institution after being reconvicted, eight were in borstal and three in prison. Of the remainder, one-fifth was known to be living in the family group. It was not possible to find out where the others were living.

The provisions for after-care embodied in the Criminal Justice Act, 1961 are not yet effective so that these men left the centres without the benefit of statutory after-care. Some were offered and accepted voluntary after-care. This acceptance, however, did not always mean that the man actually sought the help of his after-care supervisor. Others were still subject to the supervision of a probation officer under an existing probation order. The information on this point was far from clear and the evidence of an existing probation order had to be deduced from evidence of previous convictions and sentences. Subject to this qualification the evidence shows that approximately one in four of the men could call on the help of an after-care supervisor or probation officer.

The research workers completed their study of these 101 men sentenced to detention in these two centres when they had obtained final details of reconvictions in January 1961 and the limitations in their knowledge of what happened to the men after their discharge were accepted as part of the research scheme. The conclusions which are set out in the following chapter are based on the study of these men inside the centres, on what is known of the detention centre system itself as it operated in England and Wales during the period September 1960 to March 1962.

CHAPTER SEVEN

SUMMARY AND CONCLUSIONS

THE aim of this study has been to learn something of the attitudes of these young men and their reaction to detention centre training. In setting out their conclusions the research workers are aware of the limitations imposed by the objectives of the research and by the size of the sample which had to be kept small enough for each man to be personally known to the research workers. It was never intended, nor would it have been possible, to submit to exacting statistical evaluation the ill-expressed and sometimes confused attitudes and reactions of a group of offenders sentenced to detention in a detention centre. Moreover, the size of the sample did not provide the level of confidence in observed phenomena that can be obtained from larger numbers. Nevertheless, some comment on observed differences and similarities is justifiable when they follow a consistent pattern, and certain patterns did emerge when the men gave consistent answers to a series of questions. With these qualifications, the following summary of their observations and the most significant conclusions from them are offered by the research workers after close study of a sample group of offenders subjected to a detention centre sentence and observation of the working of the detention centre system in all the senior centres in England and Wales.

The punishment of young offenders by detention in a detention centre is a new method of dealing with those who have been found guilty of a breach in the criminal law. From the outset the professed aim of this sentence was deterrence, both in the sense of preventing the individual offender from committing further offences by making him afraid of further punishment and in the more general sense of deterring potential offenders by holding out the threat of what might happen to them. In due course, however, the need for training, even within the framework of a punitive sentence was acknowledged. There have, therefore, been some changes that produced a different atmosphere in the centres but the regimen has remained substantially the same since the first detention centre was opened.

The Criminal Justice Act of 1948 explicitly excluded from such punishment those who had already been sentenced to borstal training or imprisonment. The courts were also forbidden by statute to send to detention those who could properly be dealt with by discharge, fine, probation, or attendance centre. They are discouraged also, by successive Home Office circulars, from using this form of punishment for those who have not responded to longer training and those whose offences could be ascribed to personal difficulties of a serious kind. In the years 1959 and 1960[1] courts throughout the country used the sentence of detention principally for offenders who do not seem well-versed in crime and for those whose offences are not regarded as particularly serious—those who have been found guilty of offences of violence and of certain breaches of the Road Traffic Acts are cases in point. There are, however, among those sentenced to detention, some young men who have never been found guilty by a court before and others who have a long history of offences and of long-term corrective treatment that has had no effect.

In the type of offence committed and the number of previous convictions recorded against them, the sample group of offenders interviewed by the research workers at two selected detention centres closely resembles the total number of offenders committed to all senior detention centres in 1959 and 1960. It is probable that the sample is, in other respects also, similar to the total population of the detention centres in these years. The sample group shows a high degree of illegitimacy, of absence from the family home, of unsatisfactory family relationships, of poor educational attainment and of employment that was sporadic, aimless and sometimes dull. Except for a small number of apprentices, these young men were paid fairly high wages, of which a considerable proportion was at their own disposal. Periods of unemployment, however, reduced the amount of money that was available to them and few, if any, had much to spare. Drinking was common and, although there is little evidence of

[1] There have been changes in the pattern of committals in the year 1961. These are discussed later in this chapter.

serious drunkenness, it is clear that certain offences, violence and taking and driving particularly, were committed when the men had consumed a little more than was usual for them. One curious fact emerged that was quite unexpected.[2] The offenders who were sentenced to detention by midland and northern courts were different in many ways from those who came from the south. The men at the Werrington centre were more honest but more violent, more attached to their families and homes, more able and willing to keep their jobs than those who were interviewed at Aylesbury. They were different too in their attitude to their sentence and its consequences, to the function of the staff and so on. This general distinction between offenders in the north and those in the south was confirmed in discussions with wardens and chief officers in other centres in the northern half of England.

At their first interview with the research workers the men appeared to be subdued and apprehensive, although there were some who were aggrieved and resentful. They thought of their sentence simply as a punishment designed to deter themselves and others from further offences. The majority did not think it likely that they would learn anything save that they should not offend again. They expressed great dislike of individual items in the regimen—early rising, constant changing, food and the no-smoking rule. They recalled with particular distaste their reception into the centre, for they were convinced that it was planned and designed to frighten and subdue them. Their attitude to the officers was coloured by this belief, so that, although they were prepared to concede that the staff had a certain job to do, they would not help them in this task by seeking or accepting friendly relations with them.

The staff at the centres of Werrington and Aylesbury seemed to have a clear idea of the kind of offenders they might expect to receive at the centres. The typical detention centre inmate was immature, badly brought up, ill-mannered, self-pitying, stupid, resentful and bumptious—never very tough or aggressive. It is not easy to see whether this picture of the typical inmate is one that the staff had built up from official and judicial pronouncements on the type of offender who should be sent to detention

[2]This could not have been due to the design of the experiment. Two research workers conducted the enquiry both at Werrington and Aylesbury and the men were allocated for interview to each by random selection.

or upon their experience of those who responded best to the detention centre itself. Staff reports on the inmates showed a certain amount of sympathy for men with more obvious difficulties but they were not always able to diagnose what the real reasons for these difficulties were. If a man conformed and his performance and behaviour were up to standard, the staff had neither the time nor the opportunity to observe whether the sentence was useful or harmful.

There was a considerable change in the men's attitude when their sentence was nearly over and they were ready for discharge. Dislike of individual parts of the regime had been replaced by dislike of detention in itself and the loss of freedom which this entailed. This was, for them, the whole burden of the sentence and they had no desire to repeat it. They gave a reasonable account of some of the constructive parts of the sentence—evening classes and so on. It became clear that the opportunities for real training afforded by the educational programme were not always fully used, so that for example, the allocation of men to particular classes was sometimes dictated by the convenience of the general programme rather than the needs of the inmate. By implication the programme of evening classes was regarded as of secondary importance to the programme of daytime activities.

The relations of the inmates with each other became a matter of great importance to them and the influence of delinquent groups and individuals was strong. The men's attitude to the officers, however, remained critical. The rigidity of the regime did not allow for the informality on which all good personal relationships are based.

Details of the later history of the 101 men who were interviewed both at the beginning and the end of their sentence were not easy to obtain and just under half were included in the review of the first six-months' period after their release. The first reconvictions are interesting in themselves. They contain more of the younger men, more dishonest offenders, more men with a long history of previous convictions than was characteristic of the group as a whole. They also contain more of the men who were assessed as 'assured' by the research workers in the period immediately following their reception into the centre. The evidence that is available of the employment history of these men after their discharge is far from encouraging, for, although jobs may be obtained with difficulty, they seem to be readily abandoned. Some of the men who gave information about themselves after their discharge had difficulties at home, with their families and with their friends so that their resettlement was clearly not easy.

During the course of this study there was no social worker on the staff of any senior detention centre. This meant that all the preparations for release had to be undertaken by wardens and staff. Administratively this was an adequate arrangement. Letters were written to probation officers, youth employment officers and so on. Each offender had a pre-release interview with the warden or his deputy where he could raise any point of difficulty that occurred to him. Generally, however, the offenders' relations with the administration were formal, and real difficulties were not always dealt with. One centre in the north had devised a liaison scheme with the probation service that seemed to be working well. A probation officer from the probation area in which the centre lay is given the special task of preparing the men for release. There are, as yet, no concrete results of this scheme to offer as evidence of its success or failure although the warden is convinced that the scheme is working well. The research workers, however, felt that much more needed to be done in the preparation of the offenders for their release. The appointment of a fully trained social worker to each senior detention centre should do much to meet this need if such a social worker is given the opportunity of helping to resolve the personal and environmental difficulties of each offender throughout the whole period of his sentence and particularly before his release.

Since the opening of the first detention centre, the absence of any adequate system of after-care has been one of the principal objections to them. The Criminal Justice Act of 1961 makes provision for statutory after-care but this has not yet been brought into effect. It is essential that young offenders released from this kind of punitive detention should be given support and help in the period immediately following their release.

At the end of their task the research workers had reached certain conclusions about the sentence of detention in its present form that may be of some relevance in making the adjustments in this sentence that may be necessary as a consequence of the Criminal Justice Act of 1961.

1. All the evidence shows that the punitive and deterrent effect of detention in a detention centre is due to the enforced deprivation of liberty.

The elements in the sentence that are avowedly penal could be mitigated without any loss in the effectiveness of the deterrent power of the sentence. This would make it possible to introduce more constructive measures and to make the regimen less rigid and formal. This applies to the programme of work, to the disciplinary role of the staff, and the formality of the regimen as a whole.

2. The careful selection of offenders for this short-term sentence is of the greatest importance. The Criminal Justice Act provides that when sufficient accommodation is available, all short-term sentences for offenders between seventeen and twenty-one will be served in detention centres. It is not easy to see that careful selection will then be possible. Yet it would be regrettable if the principles of selecting offenders for this form of punishment, recommended by the Magistrates' Association and laid down in Home office circulars had to be abandoned.

3. In any classification of offenders sentenced to detention, provision should be made to maintain the regional basis of the present detention centre system in view of the differences between northern and southern offenders.

4. The need for preparation for release and adequate after-care is stressed once again.

5. There is little evidence to suggest that the present sentences of longer than three months are anything but an administrative difficulty. From the point of view of the offender they do not seem to be harmful. Offenders committed for non-payment of fines are not amenable to detention centre training.

There are many other points of detail on which the research workers felt that it might be possible to comment, but, with the coming into force of the Criminal Justice Act of 1961, a new chapter in the history of detention centres has begun. There has already been a rapid extension in this form of punishment so that it is possible that the whole shape of the sentence may be changed.

Among the developments that have taken place, one of the most significant has been the change in the type of young man committed to the senior centres. In 1961, 35 per cent. of them had a record of more than four previous offences, as compared with 12 per cent. in earlier years. In view of the recommendations of the Magistrates' Association and the guidance given in Home Office circulars, this change in the composition of the detention centre population should be carefully watched. The observations of the research workers engaged on this study confirms the belief that the more sophisticated offenders exert a considerable influence over those who are less delinquent. This may be due to the relative youth and inexperience of those who are committed to senior detention centres.

It may not be possible to ensure that the young man of many offences is kept out of the detention centres as they are at present constituted. Legislative provision, however, could be made for the younger offenders by implementing the Criminal Justice Act of 1961 by stages so that, for sentences up to six months, imprisonment would no longer be an alternative to detention first for those of seventeen years, then of eighteen, then nineteen and so on. The centres might then be able to adapt themselves to all ages or else they could be classified for individual age-groups.

Other changes may take place in the population of senior detention centres, yet the conclusions of the research workers, that these institutions may have some value for a small proportion of offenders, the younger and less sophisticated, appear to be valid until further research upon the changed type of detention centres makes other conclusions imperative.

TWO CASE STUDIES

Case I. J.B. aged 18 years 11 months.

Offence: Assault occasioning actual bodily harm (to a policeman).

This man came from a delinquent area of a big city. He was a tall loose-limbed and rather round-shouldered looking boy with a childish, chubby face, watery blue eyes and weak, full lips. He was friendly and quite well-spoken but at the first interview he was very tearful and distressed by any mention of home.

Family
He is the elder of two boys from a well-respected family who live in a slum area but have a well kept, clean terrace house. The father had been in his employment as a transport worker all his working life. The mother was said, by the boy's schoolmaster, to be slightly neurotic and fond but over-indulgent of her children. It appears to be a happy family. J.B. had never been away from home before. He is fond of his mother and father and admires the latter particularly for his steady work record. He seeks advice from his father and was punished by him, sometimes being given a 'good hiding'. Both parents were very upset by his offence and he says that his mother 'has not been the same since'. Questions about home provoked floods of tears so that his answers were brief. His mother and friend visited him on one occasion at the centre and his father and brother on another.

School
He attended a secondary modern school and left from the top class. His ability was said to be 'quite good', his behaviour 'reasonable' and his attendance satisfactory.

Associates and leisure at home
He does not appear to have had a girl-friend at this time but had one close mate. He admitted to being 'a bit of a Ted' and, according to the police and the school, his friends were 'the wrong sort', noisy and disorderly. He disapproves of 'loafing Teds'. According to his probation officer, he spends much time at home and he himself said he read a lot. But he also goes to the pictures once or twice a week, has a drink on Fridays, Saturdays and Sundays and dances once or twice a week. His only other leisure activity

was street football. His first evening away from the centre he expected to spend at home after he had seen his friend.

He said he spent about £100 a year on clothes, a fair amount on drink and smoked twenty or more cigarettes a day. At his last job he earned £9 and gave his mother at least £5 for his board.

Work

According to his probation officer he had a 'slightly unstable work record'. He had had six jobs since leaving school chiefly as a van or errand boy. His current job was as 'second man' on a lorry. He had only had this job, at his father's place of work, for a month and the employer said it was too early to assess his work but they were prepared to re-employ him. He had been sacked twice from other jobs for 'messing around' and said he was often late. He had left two jobs for better wages but had only a maximum of four weeks unemployment in a bad work area. He had stayed for a year as a driver's mate and his ambition is to become a driver. He is returning to his father's firm.

Record

14½ years—Larceny growing fruit—Conditional discharge.
19½ years—Breaking and entering and larceny—Probation 2 years.

In the first offence he stole apples in company with several others. In the second, with four others he had been out in the country and, on the way back, they were thirsty so broke into a public house, took cigarettes and cordials and then boarded the bus home. They had no money for their fares so had to get off and were caught.

Present offence

He was originally charged with 'Grievous bodily harm' but this was reduced. The police reported that the man was leaving a dance hall when disorderly behaviour occurred. A youth was arrested and while the constable was struggling with his prisoner on the pavement J.B. kicked the policeman causing injuries to his face and mouth. The constable was still off sick as a result of his injuries several weeks later.

The man alleged that when he came out of the dance hall after some drink but not drunk, he was speaking to a friend in a car and a scuffle began opposite. He saw a policeman being beaten up by a couple of youths wearing blue serge suits similar to his own. As he stood looking in a shop window, he said that a policeman 'bashed him with a baton' and bundled him into a van. He alleged that he had twelve witnesses to prove that he was not involved in the kicking with which he was accused but that he had been told by the police that if he pleaded guilty they would reduce the charge.

Like several of those interviewed, although he denied his part in the offence he was not unduly resentful of his sentence and from this fact and from the answers to other questions it seems likely that he was more involved than he admitted.

Sentence

He thought detention was the right punishment for him—'it will straighten me out, but it is a bit too long' and he confirmed this on second interview.

He had heard of detention before and that it was 'worse than anywhere'. He would have preferred borstal except for the length because 'you are not pushed around' and smoking is allowed. His eleven days in prison had been preferable for the same reasons and because he had a cell to himself. Probation had been very helpful to him. He had completed a two year order four months previously and had a good report. The probation officer said that the offence was out of character. Another officer presented the report to the court and J.B. blames him for his sentence as he reputedly said nothing more could be done for the man. At first interview he thought that detention was suitable only for 'tough fellows' but, by the second, thought it the most effective deterrent. If it did not deter, nothing would. He suggested that there should be nine months of detention centre regime instead of borstal as it was not right to graduate to something less severe where, for example, smoking was allowed and there was no 'rough P.T.'. He did not 'fancy' corporal punishment but imagined it would be an effective deterrent for himself and others.

Training

He clearly found the whole experience of detention difficult. At first, he was tearful, miserable and very homesick. He disliked the speed and said the older inmates 'put the wind up' the newer arrivals about circuit training which he found 'terrible'. He complained that they did P.T. with the snow up the wall. None of the officers were fair except one who was leaving but that it might be possible to be friendly with them if 'you did things the way they want' or if 'you were good at P.T.'. However, by the second interview he conceded that the majority of the officers were 'all right', especially his party officer. There were two who, he said, shouted and 'picked on him'. He still detested circuit training which he thought was 'murder' and 'doing everything on the double'.

His record at the centre was rather poor. He earned the reputation of being dull and lazy. He was poor at physical activities. Only his work officer, whom he admired, gave him a good rating. He had been initially reported as a 'rather dull, frightened rabbit, nervous and unable to stay still. Should settle later' but other officers said 'he pretends to be silly to cover a sly streak' and that he was a 'clown'. He gained grade II at the first attempt but was not awarded grade III, and was, in fact, threatened with the loss of grade II and remission for laziness. He did not agree with this criticism. He did not, however, lose any remission but had a warden's report for laziness and had had extra work for petty misdemeanours—singing, leaning on his brush at work and eating his bread before his meal.

Criminality

At first interview he was not able to think of any offence of which he disapproved but, at the end of his training, he said he did not really consider himself a criminal like those who broke and entered houses—'violence is only losing your temper for a couple of minutes'. He blames the young police for any increases in violence—'they shove you around'. He admitted there were many fights in his neighbourhood some of which were started by youths 'looking at each other'. He regarded himself as much the same as the other inmates in terms of criminality. He thought offences 'for fun' should be severely dealt with.

He was one of the few who accepted after-care. He did not, however, reply to the follow-up letter. He is not thought to have been reconvicted.

He was chiefly noticeable, on interview, for his tearfulness and weakness. Despite his poor showing at the centre, he appeared to have taken his training seriously. He thought he had learned his lesson and that he must behave or else 'be back at the centre (which he hated) or somewhere tougher'. He admitted that he had now learned to behave whereas he used to 'act soft' and take nothing seriously. His friends at the centre were not too criminally involved. In view of his hitherto mild record, in the face of a highly delinquent area, he should succeed.

Case II. A.M. aged 19 years 8 months.

Offence: Breaking and entering.

This man was mature-looking, sophisticated and confident. Of middle height and stocky build, he had a good face with clear skin and an intelligent expression. He wore expensive-looking spectacles and was obviously proud of his appearance, for even his detention centre uniform was worn with an air. He described to the research worker who interviewed him the kind of clothes he usually wore and so vivid was this description that, in writing an account of him later, the research worker found it impossible to envisage him in detention centre uniform but only wearing the smart shirts and suits that he claimed to possess.

Family
He lived with his parents, a young sister and a grandfather in a comfortable house which was being bought by the family. The father was a foreman in a large factory and the mother, too, went out to work. He said he was fond of his mother and admired his father but could not get on with his grandfather. It was perhaps for this reason that he joined the army as a boy entrant immediately he left school. He was discharged at the end of $2\frac{1}{2}$ years but there is no information about the reason for this. He professed to accept the discipline of his father but a letter from his father in the man's file suggested that the relations between father and son were very strained. The father was not prepared to tolerate his son's behaviour.

School
The man attended a secondary modern school and left at fifteen. He was probably capable of more than his schooling suggested but his educational level was low. The letter he returned at the end of the research period was ill-spelt and badly couched.

Leisure
After leaving the army at the age of $17\frac{1}{2}$ he was taken up by a group of older men who made their living by house-breaking. He joined them

and found that he could make a very adequate living this way. He therefor gave up his job in a garage but pretended to his family that he was still at work. At first, most of his time was spent loafing around during the day, and housebreaking at night. Later, however, the group came to the conclusion that they were not getting enough sleep, so they decided to restrict their activities to the daytime. The young man now in the detention centre was probably valuable as a decoy. He would go up to the house they had chosen to rob, and ring the bell. If it was answered he would make some excuse, saying he was representative for a firm producing some consumer goods and so on.

When they were not housebreaking the men enjoyed a life of leisure, haunting cafés, hiring cars, generally idling around in an expensive kind of way. The offender who was being interviewed confessed that he had been experimenting with drugs to add stimulus to his already exciting life.

Work
After leaving the army he had several jobs of short duration usually as a garage mechanic. He gave this up for housebreaking.

Previous record
There was only one previous conviction (for shop-breaking) recorded against him. It is clear, however, that he had committed many other offences but was not caught.

For this conviction he was put on probation for two years. The probation officer confessed himself unable to understand the young man. He had a good home and parents who tried hard to understand their son's difficulties.

In view of his record and of his undiscovered crimes the young man was quite prepared to accept the detention centre sentence. He had a clear idea of what it was intended to do, although he thought it might be more useful for tough Teddy boys (which he was not). He said that the period in the detention centre 'made a break anyway'.

He was fairly happy, although he disliked early morning P.T., and he was intelligent and interested enough to enjoy evening classes. One reason for his contentment may have been that one of his co-offenders (an older man) was sentenced to twelve months imprisonment.

He was tolerant of the prison officers, and said that although some of them 'bawled a lot' he would be prepared to make friends with one or two of the younger ones. (It is probable that his early attitude to the prison officers was derived from a period of two months remand spent in prison.)

At the second interview he gave considerable thought to the question 'What are they trying to teach you here?' He replied 'The officers don't know or don't agree about what they are trying to teach.'

Criminality
He did not think he was a criminal himself, nor did he think that there were any real criminals at the centre. Criminals were people who could not be taught a lesson and he was sure that detention centres would teach the men in them the lesson that they must not offend again. Later, however, a reply

was received to the follow-up enquiry from this young man. He was unemployed, after having had two jobs in the four months since his discharge. Moreover, he had been before the court again for driving his employer's vehicle without an insurance.

FORMS USED IN THE ENQUIRY

Form I: Questions asked at the first interview.
Form II: Questions answered by prison officers.
Form III: Questions asked at second interview.
Form IV: Enquiry sent to all the men included in the survey.

I. DETENTION CENTRE QUESTIONNAIRE

1. Where do you live?
   (i.e. type of neighbourhood)
   How long have you lived there?
   Do you like the area?
   What sort of house do you live in?

2. With whom do you live?
   Composition of family (i.e. number of sibs. etc.)

3. Do you think you get on well together as a family?

4. Have you ever lived away from home? Where? At what age? How long? Happy/unhappy or didn't mind?

5. Who is the person—	in the family	Other
of whom you are most fond		
whom you dislike most		
whom you admire most		
who you think is a no-good, worthless type		

6. Who corrected you at home when you did wrong? and what did you do when told off?

7. When your family heard about your present offence what did they say or do? and what do they think about your being here?

    Mother

    Father

    Other

8. Who do you usually go around with at home? Who decides what you will do or where you will go?

9. With what person do you discuss important decisions to do with your life?

10. Do you have any ambition or something you long for in your life?

11. Describe the offence for which you were sent to D/C.
    (Note—who with? planned or not? reason? general circumstances.)

12. Had your heard about D/C? What? Who from?

13. Do you think D/C was the right punishment for your offence? If NOT what other punishment do you think would have been more suitable?

14. Would you rather have been sent to Borstal? Why or why not?

15. Apart from the length of time do you know anyway in which Borstal differs from D/C?

16. Have you been in prison?.... If yes, in what way does the D/C appear to differ from your experience of prison?

17. Have you ever been on probation?.... Why do you think it was necessary for you to be sent away from home this time rather than (further) supervision at home?

18. Is there anyone you can think of that you think D/C training would do good to? (describe type).

19. Is there any kind of crime or offence which you think is mean and rotten and that you would never dream of doing?

20. Describe what you did yesterday from the time you got up. Say why you think each activity is included in the programme and how you feel about each thing mentioned.

then add any of the following omitted above (P.T., marching, work, leisure activities, kit inspections, Reports, meal routine).

21. Is there anything in the programme you think ought to be changed?

22. Is there anything which you dislike at the Centre?

23. Is there anything that is better than you thought it would be?

24. How do you feel most of the time since you have been here? (Miserable, bored, frightened, fairly happy....).

25. What is the moan or complaint that you hear most from the men who have been here longer than you?

26. Do you find the officers on the whole—severe, soft, decent, fair?.... Do you think it will be possible to make friends with any of them?

27. Do you think you are likely to get into trouble again when you go home?.... Why or why not?

28. What do you think the chief thing you are going to learn here is which will help to keep you out of trouble when you go home?

29. What jobs have you had since leaving school?
    (Note—reason for leaving, whether job liked or not, timekeeping, any periods of unemployment, ability to get on with workmates, attitude to boss/foreman etc.)

30. Did any of these jobs satisfy you? Which? or if not what do you really think you want to do?

---

31. How much did you earn at your last job?
How much did you give your mother or pay for lodgings?
How much (approx.) did you spend on
    clothes
    cigarettes
    drink
    records
    in cafés
    entertainment?

II. OFFICER'S REPORT

NAME............... NUMBER...... OFFICER REPORTING......

1. Intelligence.
    (a) Is he brighter than most D/C boys?
    (b) Is he much the same as most?
    (c) Is he noticeably less intelligent than most?

2. Physical Proficiency. (P.E.I. only.)
    (a) Is he an able performer at all physical activities?
    (b) Is he an average performer?
    (c) Does he have difficulty in performing practical tasks?

3. Practical Ability. (Party Officer only.)
    (a) Is he quick and skilful at practical jobs?
    (b) Is he normally competent?
    (c) Does he have difficulty in performing practical tasks?

4. Order and Instructions.
    (a) Does he obey quickly and willingly?
    (b) Does he do what is required without getting into trouble?
    (c) Does he obey slowly and resentfully?

5. Comprehension.
    (a) Does he immediately understand all he is asked to do?
    (b) Does he have average understanding?
    (c) Does he have difficulty understanding what is expected of him?

6. Effort.
    (a) Does he make the maximum effort all the time?
    (b) Does he make an adequate effort?
    (c) Does he make the minimum effort most of the time?

7. Relationship With Other Boys.
    (a) Is he popular with the other boys?
    (b) Is he generally acceptable to the others?
    (c) Is he unpopular or unacceptable?

8. Relationshp With Officers.
    (a) Is he respectful, co-operative and responsive?
    (b) Is he normally co-operative?
    (c) Is he surly and/or unco-operative?

9. Attitude on Admission. Would you say this boy in the *first* 2–3 weeks after his admission was UNUSUALLY—homesick; frightened, anxious; surly; aggressive; resentful, cheeky, swaggering, nervous, bewildered; tough; happy-go-lucky; anxious to please;.....................
    ....(any other observation).

10. Criminality: From your observation of this boy do you gain the impression that:
    (a) He is criminal or delinquent in outlook?
    (b) He is only mildly delinquent?

    and: Would you say that, taken all round, he is the type of lad you have come to expect to deal with at the D/C?
    If no, *why*?.....................................Yes/No.

11. Improvement during training
    (a) Would you say that he has shown considerable improvement.
    (b) Has he tended to remain the same?
    (c) Has he deteriorated since being here?
    If (a) or (c), please say in what particular aspect.................

12. Length of Training?
    (a) Do you think he is ready for discharge now?
    (b) Could he have been discharged earlier?
    (c) Do you think he requires further D/C training?

13. Would you rate this boy's chances of SUCCESS (that is, keeping out of serious trouble) after he leaves here as—

GOOD   MODERATE   POOR

III. SECOND INTERVIEW

NAME.................................

1. When are you leaving?
2. Where going to?
3. Will you stay there?
4. What will you do about work?
5. What will you do first night home?
6. What are you looking forward to most? What have you missed most?
7. Have you a particular mate/friend to meet?
8. Imagine you are describing D/C to friend—what would you tell them?
9. What would you say about your officers?
10. Is there anyone/anything which you have found particularly helpful?
11. What would you say was the chief reason for avoiding being sent to a D/C?
12. What would you most dislike to come back to?
13. Do you think you have learned anything? What are they trying to teach?
14. Do you find the other men friendly/unfriendly? Have you made any close friends?
15. Compared with other men.
    (a) Do you think you are the same sort of chap?
    (b) Do you think your record/offences are the same as most?
    (c) Do you feel you were sent to the right place?
16. What sort of things do you talk about mostly among yourselves?
17. What is the chief moan/complaint?
18. What punishments have you received?
19. What letters received/written?
    Visits?
    Grades achieved?
20. How have you felt most of the time here?
21. Do you think you will get into trouble again when you leave? Why or why not?
22. Are there many fights in your home neighbourhood? What sort? When would you join in?
23. What do you think is the best way of stopping young chaps from getting into repeated trouble?
24. Why do you think men with bad records suddenly stop committing offences?
25. Do you think flogging/birching would deter you? Would do any good?
26. Why do you think so many more cases of violence and assault in the last few years?
27. What is your opinion of the police? Why?
28. If you were a magistrate/judge, what punishment would you give—
    (a) Young man who had assaulted and robbed a shopkeeper?
    (b) Young man who had broken and entered house to steal (first offence)?
    (c) Young man who *repeatedly* steals small things?

(d) Young man like yourself with your record and offences?
29. (a) Are you a criminal?
 (b) Who do you think is a criminal?
 (c) Are there any here?

IV. FOLLOW-UP ENQUIRY

When you have read the questions please put a TICK *against* YES *or* NO—*whichever fits.*

1. What is your present job?
2. Is this the job you got when you came home?   Yes ....
     No ....
3. Is it the one you had before you went away?   Yes ....
     No ....
4. How many jobs have you had since you came home? 1—2—3—4—5—
5. Have you been sacked from any?   Yes ....
     No ....
6. Do you like your present job?   Yes ....
     No ....
7. Do you think you will stay at it?   Yes ....
     No ....
8. What is your wage? £....s....d.... per week (approximately).
9. Are you satisfied with this wage?   Yes ....
     No ....
10. Have you stayed at................?   Yes ....
     No ....
11. If you have left?
     When? date............
     Why? disagreement with mother, father, any one else.
         for work
         any other reason
12. Have you had any difficulties since your return—
     at work?   Yes ....
           No ....
     with your friends?   Yes ....
           No ....
     at home?   Yes ....
           No ....
     with your girl?   Yes ....
           No ....
     with the police?   Yes ....
           No ....
     any other difficulties? Yes ....
           No ....
13. Have you had to go to court for any reason?   Yes ....
     No ....

     If YES—what reason?

14. Do you NOW think your period away did you any good? Yes ....
    No ....

15. Do you have any special plans for your future? For example—
    Marriage................
    Change of job............
    Moving from home......
    Joining Army............
        M.N.............
    Any other ....
        ....

THE DETENTION CENTRE RULES

Made 28th July, 1952
Coming into Operation 31st *July,* 1952
In pursuance of the power conferred on me by section fifty-two of the
Criminal Justice Act, 1948(**a**), I hereby make the following Rules:—

Interpretation

1.—(1) These Rules apply to Detention Centres (hereinafter referred to
as 'Centres') and to persons required to be detained therein (hereinafter
referred to as 'inmates').

(2) In these Rules unless the context otherwise requires words and expressions have the meanings respectively assigned to them as follows:—

'Chaplain' means a clergyman appointed under the Prison Acts, 1865
and 1877(**b**);

'Commissioners' means the Prison Commissioners, and 'Assistant
Commissioner' means a person appointed by the Secretary of State to
assist the Prison Commissioners and to be an inspector of prisons;

'Compulsory school age' has the meaning assigned to it by subsection
(5) of section eighteen of the Criminal Justice Act, 1948;

'Junior Centre' and 'Senior Centre' have the meanings assigned to
them by Rule 3;

'Legal adviser' means, in relation to an inmate, the inmate's counsel
or solicitor, and includes a clerk authorized by his counsel or solicitor to
interview the inmate;

'Minister' means a person appointed under section three of the Prison
Ministers Act, 1863(**c**), as amended by the Prison Acts, 1865 to 1898;

'Offence' has the meaning assigned to it by Rule 31;

'Officer' means an officer or servant of a Centre;

'Restricted diet' has the meaning assigned to it by sub-paragraph (*h*)
of paragraph (2) of Rule 32;

'Warden' and 'Deputy Warden' mean an officer appointed under
the Prison Acts, 1865 to 1898, who is assigned by the Commissioners to
take charge of a Centre or to act as deputy to an officer so assigned.

(3) Reference to the Church of England include, in relation to a Centre
situated in Wales or an inmate who is a member of the Church in Wales,
reference to the Church in Wales.

155

(4) The Interpretation Act, 1889(**d**), shall apply to the interpretation of these Rules as it applies to the interpretation of an Act of Parliament.

Citation and commencement

2. These Rules may be cited as the Detention Centre Rules, 1952, and shall come into operation on the thirty-first day of July, 1952.

CLASSIFICATION AND GRADING

Classification

3.—(1) An inmate shall be detained in that one of the four following types of Centre appropriate to his or her age and sex, namely—

(*a*) junior Centre for males under the age of seventeen;
(*b*) junior Centre for females under the age of seventeen;
(*c*) senior Centre for males aged seventeen or over;
(*d*) senior Centre for females aged seventeen or over:

Provided that a person under the age of seventeen may be detained in a senior Centre and a person aged seventeen or over may be detained in a junior Centre if in either case the Prison Commissioners, having regard to the persons' mental or physical development, so direct.

(2) A senior and a junior Centre for persons of the same sex may be in the same building.

Grading

4.—(1) On arrival at a Centre an inmate shall be placed in Grade I.

(2) Subject to any general directions by the Commissioners, an inmate may be promoted from Grade I to Grade II—

(*a*) after being not less than four weeks in Grade I, or, in the case of an inmate ordered to be detained for a term of one month, such less period in Grade I as the Warden may determine, and
(*b*) if in the opinion of the Warden his conduct justifies the promotion.

(3) Inmates promoted to Grade II shall be given such privileges as the Commissioners from time to time determine.

ACCOMMODATION

Sleeping accommodation

5. No sleeping accommodation for inmates shall be used unless it is certified by a Commissioner or Assistant Commissioner to be of such size and to be lighted, warmed, ventilated and fitted in such a manner as is requisite for health, and when such accommodation is locked it shall be furnished with the means of enabling inmates to communicate at any time with an officer. If the certificate is cancelled, that accommodation shall not be so used unless it is again certified. The certificate shall specify the maximum number of inmates to be accommodated at any one time in any room and the number so specified shall not be exceeded without the authority of the Commissioners.

Detention rooms

6. No room shall be used as a detention room for the confinement of an inmate in pursuance of a disciplinary award under Rule 32 or Rule 33 or

for the confinement of a refractory or violent inmate under Rule 38, unless
it is certified by a Commissioner or Assistant Commissioner to be suitable for
the purpose and to be furnished with the means of enabling the inmate so
confined to communicate at any time with an officer.

Beds and bedding

7. Every inmate shall be provided with a separate bed and with separate
bedding adequate for warmth and health.

RECEPTION AND REMOVAL
(i) *Reception*

Search

8.—(1) Every inmate shall be searched by an officer on reception at a
Centre, and at such subsequent times as may be directed, and all unauthorized articles shall be taken from him.

(2) The searching of an inmate shall be conducted in as seemly a manner
as is consistent with the necessity of discovering any concealed article.

(3) No inmate shall be stripped and searched in the sight of another
inmate.

(4) An inmate shall be searched only by officers of the same sex as the
inmate.

Retention of property

9. All money, clothing or other effects belonging to an inmate which he
is not allowed to retain shall be placed in the custody of the Warden, who
shall keep an inventory thereof, which shall be signed by the inmate.

Recording of particulars

10.—(1) A personal record of each inmate shall be prepared and maintained in such manner as the Commissioners determine.

(2) Every inmate may be photographed on reception and subsequently,
but no copy of the photograph shall be given to a person who is not
authorized to receive it.

Interview by Warden

11. Every inmate shall as soon as possible after his reception be separately
interviewed by the Warden.

Medical examination

12. Every inmate shall, on the day of his reception, as soon as possible
after his reception, be separately examined by the Medical Officer, who
shall record the state of health of the inmate and such other particulars as
may be directed:

Provided that when an inmate is received too late to be examined on the
same day he shall be examined as soon as possible on the next day, and in
any case within twenty-four hours of reception.

Babies

13. Subject to such conditions as the Commissioners determine, a girl may
have her baby with her in the Centre during the period of lactation and

longer if required in special circumstances, and the baby may be supplied with clothing and necessaries at the public expense.

(ii) *Information to inmates*

Providing and explaining information

14. The Warden shall ensure that every inmate receives a careful explanation of so much of these Rules and of any other regulations as should be brought to his knowledge, including those relating to payments, to activities of the Centre, to the proper methods of submitting petitions to the Secretary of State and of making complaints, to food, clothing, bedding, and other necessaries, and to the disciplinary requirements of the Centre so that he may understand both his rights and his obligations.

(iii) *Removal and release*

Custody during removal, etc.

15. An inmate whom the Secretary of State has directed to be taken to any place shall while outside the Centre be kept in the custody of officers of a Centre or of prison officers:

Provided that an inmate directed to be brought before a magistrates' court may while outside the Centre be in the custody of police officers.

Protection from public view

16. When inmates are removed to or from a Centre, they shall be exposed to public view as little as possible and proper safeguards shall be adopted to protect them from insult or curiosity.

Final interview with Warden and with Medical Officer

17. An inmate shall before release or removal to any other place be interviewed by the Warden, and shall, as short a time as is practicable before release or removal to any other place, be examined by the Medical Officer, and shall not be so removed unless the Medical Officer certifies that he is fit for removal.

Return of clothes

18. On the release of an inmate, his own clothes shall be returned to him unless it has been found necessary to destroy or otherwise dispose of them, in which case proper clothing shall be provided.

(iv) *Deaths of inmates*

Record of death

19. The Medical Officer shall keep a record of the death of an inmate which shall include the following particulars:—

At what time the deceased was taken ill, when the illness was first notified to the Medical Officer, the nature of the illness, when the inmate died, and an account of the appearance after death (in cases where a *post mortem* examination is made), together with any special remarks that appear to the Medical Officer to be required.

The Detention Centre Rules

Notice to Coroner, etc.

20. Upon the death of an inmate the Warden shall give immediate notice thereof to the Coroner having jurisdiction, to the Board of Visitors, and to the Commissioners.

DISCIPLINE AND CONTROL

(i) *General*

Inspection

21. Centres shall be open to inspection at all times by and on behalf of the Commissioners and by inspectors designated for the purpose on behalf of the Secretary of State.

Supervision by Warden

22.—(1) The Warden shall exercise a close and constant personal supervision of the whole Centre. He shall visit and inspect daily all parts of the Centre where inmates are working or accommodated, and shall give special attention to every inmate who is sick.

(2) At least twice a fortnight the Warden shall during the night visit the Centre and satisfy himself as to its state.

Performance of Warden's duties by other persons

23.—(1) The Warden may depute any officer to act in his stead in his absence, and that officer shall in the Warden's absence perform all the duties of the Warden.

(2) The Warden may delegate to the Deputy Warden (if any) such duties as from time to time the Commissioners approve.

Supervision, etc., of girls

24. Girls shall be attended only by women officers and if working under a male instructor shall be supervised by a woman officer.

Use of force

25.—(1) No officer in dealing with inmates shall use force unnecessarily and, when the application of force to an inmate is necessary, no more force than is necessary shall be used.

(2) No officer shall deliberately act in a manner calculated to provoke an inmate.

(ii) *Remission*

Conditions of remitting sentence

26. Arrangements shall be made by which an inmate ordered to be detained for a period exceeding one month may by good conduct and industry become eligible for release when a portion of his term of detention not exceeding one-sixth of the whole term of detention has yet to run.

(iii) *Offences against discipline*

Warden to deal with reports

27. No report against an inmate shall be dealt with by any officer except the Warden, or an officer who by virtue of Rule 23 has authority to deal with such reports.

Separation of reported inmates

28. When an inmate has been reported for an offence the Warden may order him to be kept apart from other inmates pending adjudication.

Information to reported inmate

29. An inmate shall, before a report against him is dealt with, be informed of the offence for which he has been reported and shall be given a proper opportunity of hearing the facts alleged against him and of presenting his case.

Unauthorized articles

30. The Warden may deprive an inmate of any unauthorized article found in his room or in his possession.

Offences

31. An inmate whose behaviour is such as to offend against the good order and discipline of the Centre may be punished by the Warden or the Board of Visitors in the manner provided by these Rules.

Investigation of offences, and awards, by Warden

32.—(1) Every offence shall be reported forthwith, and the Warden shall investigate the report not later than the following day, unless that day is a Sunday or a public holiday.

(2) If upon investigation the Warden considers that the offence is proved, he shall (subject to the provisions of Rule 33) make one or more of the following awards:—

(*a*) caution;

(*b*) removal for a period not exceeding fourteen days from such activity or activities of the Centre, other than work, as are specified in the award;

(*c*) extra work or fatigues outside normal working hours, for not more than two hours on any one day and for a period not exceeding fourteen days;

(*d*) stoppage of payments under paragraph (2) of Rule 47 for a period not exceeding fourteen days;

(*e*) reduction to Grade I;

(*f*) removal to a detention room for a period not exceeding fourteen days under such restrictions of activities of the Centre (including work) and with such stoppage of payments under paragraph (2) of Rule 47 as the Commissioners shall have determined;

(*g*) confinement to a detention room for a period not exceeding twenty-four hours in a junior Centre and three days in a senior Centre;

(*h*) restricted diet upon a scale approved by the Commissioners for a period not exceeding three days in a junior Centre and seven days in a senior Centre, provided that the said scale shall not be such as to reduce the offender's diet below a nutritional standard adequate for his health and strength at normal work;

(*i*) forfeiture of remission of the term of detention for a period not exceeding seven days.

The Detention Centre Rules

Investigation of offences, and awards, by Boards of Visitors

33.—(1) Where an inmate is reported for an offence upon which the Warden, having regard to the circumstances of the case, thinks it expedient that the Board of Visitors should adjudicate, the Warden may after investigation refer the case to the Board of Visitors.

(2) The Board of Visitors shall inquire into every case referred to them under the foregoing paragraph and, if they find the offence proved, shall make one or more awards authorized under paragraph (2) of Rule 32:
Provided that—

(a) an award lettered (b), (c), (d) or (f) in the said paragraph (2) may be for a period not exceeding twenty-eight days;

(b) an award of confinement to a detention room may be for a period not exceeding three days in a junior Centre and seven days in a senior Centre;

(c) an award of forfeiture of remission of the term of detention may be for a period exceeding seven days.

(3) The Warden may, notwithstanding the foregoing provisions of this Rule, refer to the Commissioners a case to which paragraph (1) of this Rule applies, and thereupon a Commissioner or Assistant Commissioner shall have authority to inquire into the case and deal with it in the same manner as the Board of Visitors.

(4) The functions of the Board of Visitors under this Rule shall be exercised by not less than two and not more than five members of the Board.

Medical certificate

34. Confinement to a detention room or restricted diet shall in no case be awarded under Rule 32 or Rule 33 unless the Medical Officer has certified that the inmate is in a fit condition of health to sustain it.

Visits by Warden and Medical Officer

35. Every inmate undergoing confinement to a detention room or subject to restricted diet in accordance with Rule 32 or Rule 33 shall be visited at least once a day by both the Warden and the Medical Officer, and if he is undergoing confinement to a detention room he shall be visited by an officer appointed for that purpose at intervals of not more than three hours during the day.

Remission and mitigation of awards

36.—(1) A disciplinary award may be determined or mitigated by the Secretary of State.

(2) A disciplinary award other than an award lettered (a) or (i) in paragraph (2) of Rule 32 may be determined or mitigated at any time during the currency thereof by the authority responsible for the award.

(iv) *Restraints*

Mechanical restraints

37.—(1) Mechanical restraints shall not be used in a junior Centre, and shall not be used in a senior Centre as a punishment or for any purpose other than safe custody during removal, except on medical grounds by direction of the Medical Officer, or in the circumstances and under the conditions stated in the following paragraphs of this Rule.

(2) When it appears to the Warden that it is necessary to place an inmate of a senior Centre under mechanical restraint in order to prevent his injuring himself or others, or damaging property, or creating a disturbance, the Warden may order him to be placed under mechanical restraint, and notice thereof shall forthwith be given to a member of the Board of Visitors and to the Medical Officer.

(3) The Medical Officer on receipt of the aforesaid notice shall forthwith inform the Warden whether he concurs in the order, and if on medical grounds he does not concur the Warden shall act in accordance with any recommendations which he makes.

(4) No inmate shall be kept under mechanical restraint longer than is necessary, or for a longer period than twenty-four hours unless an order in writing from a member of the Board of Visitors or a Commissioner or Assistant Commissioner is given, specifying the reason thereof and the time during which the inmate may be so kept, which order shall be preserved by the Warden as his warrant.

(5) Particulars of every case of mechanical restraint shall be forthwith recorded by the Warden.

(6) No mechanical means of restraint shall be used except of such patterns and in such manner and under such conditions as may be approved by the Secretary of State.

Temporary confinement

38.—(1) The Warden may order a refractory or violent inmate to be temporarily confined to a detention room, but no inmate shall be confined under this Rule to such a room after he has ceased to be refractory or violent.

(2) An inmate so confined under the foregoing paragraph shall be visited at least once a day by the Warden and the Medical Officer and at intervals of not more than three hours during the day by an officer appointed for that purpose.

(v) *Complaints by inmates*

Complaints to be recorded and put forward

39.—(1) Arrangements shall be made that every request by an inmate to see the Warden, or a Commissioner or Assistant Commissioner, or a member of the Board of Visitors, shall be recorded by the officer to whom it is made and conveyed without delay to the Warden.

(2) The Warden shall at a convenient hour on every day, other than Sundays and public holidays, hear the applications of all inmates who have made a request to see him, and shall inform the next Commissioner or Assistant Commissioner or member of the Board of Visitors who visits the Centre of every such request of an inmate to see such Commissioner or Assistant Commissioner or member.

The Detention Centre Rules

(vi) *Prohibited articles*

Prohibited articles generally

40. No person shall without authority convey into or throw into or deposit in a Centre, or convey or throw out of a Centre, or convey to an inmate, or deposit in any place with the intent that it shall come into the possession of an inmate, any money, clothing, food, drink, tobacco, letter, paper, book, tool, or other article whatever, Anything so conveyed, thrown or deposited may be confiscated by the Warden.

Drink and Tobacco

41.—(1) No inmate shall be given or allowed to have any intoxicating liquor except in pursuance of a written order of the Medical Officer specifying the quantity to be given and the name of the inmate for whose use it is intended.

(2) No inmate of a junior Centre and, except in accordance with such orders as may be given by the Warden with the approval of the Commissioners, no inmate of a senior Centre shall be allowed to smoke or to have in his possession any tobacco.

(vii) *Control of admission*

General Restrictions

42.—(1) All persons and vehicles entering or leaving the Centre may be examined and searched.

(2) A person suspected of bringing any prohibited article into the Centre, or of carrying out a prohibited article or any property belonging to the Centre, or while in a Centre of being in possession of a prohibited article, or in improper possession of any property belonging to the Centre, shall be stopped and immediate notice thereof shall be given to the Warden, who may order that he shall be examined and searched.

(3) The Warden may refuse admission to the Centre of a person who is not willing to be examined and searched.

(4) The Warden may direct the removal from the Centre of a person who while in the Centre is not willing to be examined and searched, or whose conduct is improper.

Visitors viewing Centres

43.—(1) The Warden shall not, except as provided by statute, or as directed by the Secretary of State or the Commissioners, allow any person to view the Centre.

(2) The Warden shall ensure that no person authorized to view the Centre makes a sketch, or takes a photograph or holds communication with an inmate, unless authorized to do so by the Secretary of State or the Commissioners.

EMPLOYMENT OF INMATES

Normal working week

44. The normal working week shall be forty-four hours.

Education

45.—(1) In the case of inmates of compulsory school age, arrangements shall be made for their full-time education within the normal working week.

(2) In the case of inmates not of compulsory school age, arrangements shall be made for their part-time education either within the normal working week or outside it.

Recreation

46. At least one hour a day shall be devoted to physical training or to organized games and such period shall be deemed to form part of the normal working week.

General requirements

47.—(1) The medical Officer may excuse an inmate from work or from physical training or organized games on medical grounds, and no inmate shall be employed on any work unless he has been certified as fit for that type of work by the Medical Officer.

(2) Inmates may receive payments related to their industry in accordance with rates approved by the Commissioners, and may spend money so received on such articles and subject to such conditions as the Commissioners determine.

(3) No inmate shall be set to any type of work not authorized by the Commissioners.

(4) Except with the authority of the Commissioners, no inmate shall work in the service of another inmate or of an officer or for the private benefit of any person.

RELIGION AND WELFARE

(i) *Religion*

Recording of denomination

48. The religious denomination of every inmate shall be ascertained and recorded on his reception and he shall be treated as a member of the denomination then recorded unless and until he satisfies the Board of Visitors that he has good grounds for desiring the record to be altered.

Visits by special ministers

49. Where an inmate is recorded as belonging to a religious denomination other than the Church of England for which no Minister has been appointed to the Centre, the Warden shall if the inmate so requests arrange for him, so far as possible, to be visited by a minister of that denomination, and every such inmate shall be informed of this Rule on reception.

Religious services

50.—(1) At least once on every Sunday, Christmas Day and Good Friday and on such other occasions as may be arranged, the Chaplain shall conduct for inmates belonging to the Church of England periods of religious worship or instruction.

(2) Ministers shall conduct for inmates of their denominations periods of religious worship or instruction at such times as may be arranged.

Visits by chaplain or minister

51. Every inmate shall so far as practicable be regularly visited at proper and reasonable times by the Chaplain or, if he is recorded as belonging to a denomination other than the Church of England, by a minister of his own denomination.

Religious books

52. There shall so far as practicable be available for the personal use of every inmate such of the Scriptures and books of religious observance and instruction recognized for his denomination as are accepted by the Commissioners for use in Centres.

Interviews, visits to sick, etc.

53.—(1) The Chaplain or a Minister shall—

(a) interview individually every inmate recorded as belonging to the Church of England or to that Minister's denomination, as the case may be, as soon as possible after the inmate's reception, a short time before his discharge, and from time to time as often as practicable during his detention; and

(b) if no other arrangements are made, read the burial service at the funeral of such an inmate dying in the Centre.

(2) The Chaplain shall daily visit any sick inmate who is recorded as belonging to the Church of England, and a Minister shall so far as possible do the same for any such inmate recorded as belonging to the Minister's denomination.

(3) When an inmate not recorded as belonging to the Church of England is sick and is not regularly visited by a minister of his own denomination, the Chaplain shall visit him if the inmate is willing.

Sunday work, etc.

54. Arrangements shall be made for the avoidance of all unnecessary work by inmates of the Christian religion on Sunday, Christmas Day and Good Friday, and by inmates recorded as belonging to other religions on their recognized days of religious observance.

Substitute for chaplain or minister

55.—(1) Such person as the Commissioners approve may officiate in the Chaplain's absence.

(2) A Minister may with the consent of the Commissioners appoint a substitute to act for him in his absence.

(ii) *Libraries*

Library

56. A library shall be provided in every Centre and, subject to such conditions as the Commissioners determine, every inmate shall be allowed to have library books and to exchange them as often as practicable.

(iii) *Social relations and after-care*

Family relationships, etc.

57.—(1) Special attention shall be paid to the maintenance of such

165

relations between an inmate and his family as are judged to be desirable in the best interests of the inmate.

(2) So far as is practicable and in the opinion of the Warden desirable, an inmate shall be encouraged and assisted to maintain or establish such relations with persons or agencies outside the Centre as may promote his social rehabilitation.

(3) The Warden may at any time communicate to an inmate, or to his family or friends, any matter of importance to such inmate.

After-care

58.—(1) It shall be the duty of the Board of Visitors to make such arrangements as are practicable for the after-care of inmates of the Centre who are willing to accept after-care.

(2) In discharging the said duty the Board of Visitors shall act in consultation with the Warden and with a probation officer.

Information to family of death, etc.

59. Upon the death or serious illness, or certification as insane or mentally defective, of an inmate, or the sustaining by an inmate of a serious accident, the Warden shall at once inform the nearest relative whose address is known, and shall in any event inform any other person whom the inmate has requested may be so informed.

(iv) *Letters and visits*

Normal minimum provision

60.—(1) Every inmate shall be allowed to write and receive a letter on reception and thereafter once in two weeks and to receive a visit once in four weeks:

Provided that in lieu of a visit the Warden may allow an inmate to write a letter and receive a reply.

(2) The Warden may for special reasons allow an inmate to receive or write additional letters or receive additional visits.

Letters and visits generally

61.—(1) Without prejudice to the provisions of Rule 60 the Commissioners, notwithstanding any provision of this and the following five Rules, may impose such restrictions upon and supervision over letters and visits as they consider necessary for securing discipline and good order, for the prevention of crime and criminal associations, and for the welfare of individuals.

(2) Except as provided in these Rules, no person shall be allowed to communicate with an inmate without special authority.

(3) Subject to paragraph (3) of Rule 89 every letter to or from an inmate shall be read by the Warden or by a responsible officer deputed by him for the purpose, and it shall be within the discretion of the Warden to stop any letter on the ground that its contents are objectionable or that it is of inordinate length.

(4) The degree of supervision to be exercised during visits to inmates shall, subject to any express provision of these Rules be in the discretion of the Warden.

Deferment

62. When an inmate who is entitled to a letter or visit under any provision of these Rules is at the time in a detention room under Rule 32, Rule 33 or Rule 38, the letter or visit may in the Warden's discretion be deferred until the period in the detention room has expired.

(v) *Visits for special purposes*

Visits by police

63. An officer of police may visit any inmate who is willing to see him on production of an order issued by or on behalf of the appropriate chief officer of police.

Visits by legal adviser

64.—(1) Reasonable facilities shall be allowed for the legal adviser of an inmate who is a party to legal proceedings, civil or criminal, to interview the inmate with reference to those proceedings out of the hearing of an officer.

(2) The legal adviser of an inmate may, with the permission of the Commissioners, see such inmate with reference to any other legal business.

Persons detained in default of payment

65. Where a person has been ordered to be detained in a Centre in default of the payment of a sum of money, he shall be allowed to have an interview with his friends on a week-day at any reasonable hour, or to communicate by letter with them for the purpose of providing for a payment which would procure his release from detention, and every such person shall on his reception be informed of this Rule.

Special purpose visits not to be forfeited

66. The visits and letters under Rules 63, 64 and 65 shall be additional to the visits and letters allowed under any other of the foregoing Rules.

PHYSICAL WELFARE

(i) *Medical Services*

Hospital

67.—(1) At every Centre a suitable part of the Centre shall be equipped and furnished as a sick bay for the medical care and treatment of inmates suffering from minor sicknesses.

(2) Any sick inmate for whom adequate treatment cannot be provided in the Centre shall as soon as possible be removed to a hospital.

Medical Officer; general duties

68.—(1) The Medical Officer shall have the care of the mental and physical health of the inmates.

(2) Without prejudice to the duties expressly conferred on the Medical Officer by the foregoing Rules and in particular Rules 35 and 38 the Medical Officer shall as often as is in his opinion necessary, and normally every day, visit every sick inmate in the Centre, and every other inmate to whom his attention is specially directed.

Immediate attendance and consultations

69.—(1) The Medical Officer shall attend at once on receiving information of the illness of an inmate.

(2) The Medical Officer may at his discretion call into consultation another medical practitioner.

(3) The Medical Officer shall keep a record of occasions on which in accordance with this Rule he consults another medical practitioner.

Duty to report

70. The Medical Officer shall report to the Warden any matter which appears to him to require the consideration of the Commissioners on medical grounds, and the Warden shall send such report to the Commissioners.

Report on danger to health, etc.

71. Whenever the Medical Officer has reason to believe that an inmate's mental or physical health is likely to be injuriously affected by his continued detention or by any conditions of his detention, or that the life of an inmate will be endangered by his detention or that a sick inmate will not survive his sentence or is totally or permanently unfit for Centre discipline, he shall without delay report the case in writing to the Warden with such recommendations as he thinks fit, and the Warden shall forward such report and recommendations to the Commissioners forthwith.

Recommendations on diet, etc.

72. The Medical Officer shall report in writing to the Warden the case of any inmate to which he thinks it necessary on medical grounds to draw attention, and shall make such recommendations as he deems needful for the alteration of the diet or treatment of the inmate or for his separation from other inmates, or for the supply to him of additional clothing, bedding or other articles, and the Warden shall so far as practicable carry such recommendations into effect.

Suicidal inmates

73. The Medical Officer shall draw the attention of the Warden to any inmate who he may have reason to think has suicidal intentions in order that special observation may be kept on such inmate, and the Warden shall, without delay, direct that such inmate be observed at frequent intervals.

Mental illness

74. The Medical Officer shall keep under special observation every inmate whose mental condition appears to require it, and shall take such steps as he considers proper for his segregation, and if necessary his certification under the Acts relating to lunacy or mental deficiency.

Serious illness

75. The Medical Officer shall give notice to the Warden and the Chaplain when an inmate appears to be seriously ill.

(ii) *Hygiene*

Supervision of hygiene

76. The Medical Officer shall oversee and shall advise the Warden upon the hygiene of the Centre and the inmates, including arrangements for cleanliness, sanitation, heating, lighting and ventilation.

Washing, shaving, and hair cutting
77. Arrangements shall be made for every inmate to wash at all proper times, to have a hot bath at least once a week and for male inmates (unless excused or prohibited on medical or other grounds) to shave or be shaved when necessary and to have their hair cut as required. The hair of a male inmate may be cut as short as is necessary for good appearance, but the hair of a female inmate shall not be cut without her consent, except by direction of the Medical Officer for the eradication of vermin, dirt, or disease, which direction shall be given in writing.

Toilet articles
78. Every inmate shall be provided on admission with such toilet articles as are necessary for health and cleanliness and arrangements shall be made for the replacement of those articles when necessary.

(iii) *Food*

Quality of Food
79. The food provided for inmates shall be of a nutritional value adequate for health and strength and of wholesome quality, well prepared and served, and reasonably varied.

Inspection of food
80. The Medical Officer shall frequently inspect the food, cooked and uncooked, provided for inmates, and shall report to the Warden on the state and quality of the food and on any deficiency in the quantity or defect in the quality of the water.

No private food
81. Except as determined by the Commissioners, or on medical grounds, no inmate shall be allowed to have any food other than the normal Centre diet.

Quantity of food
82. Except in the case of inmates on restricted diet, or on the written recommendation of the Medical Officer in the case of an inmate who persistently wastes his food, or on medical grounds by direction of the Medical Officer, no inmate shall have less food than is provided in the normal Centre diet.

(iv) *Clothing*

No private clothing
83. Every inmate shall be provided with an outfit of clothing adequate for warmth and health, in accordance with a scale approved by the Commissioners, and shall, except as approved by the Commissioners, wear such clothing and no other.

Protective clothing

84. The clothing provided shall, where necessary, include suitable protective clothing for use at work.

Application of rules

85. The four following Rules apply to inmates who are appellants within the meaning of the Criminal Appeal Act, 1907(**e**) (hereinafter called 'appellants').

Appellants absent from Centre

86.—(1) An appellant who, when in custody, is to be taken to, kept in custody at, or brought back from, any place at which he is entitled to be present for the purposes of the Criminal Appeal Act, 1907, or any place to which the Court of Criminal Appeal or any Judge thereof may order him to be taken for the purpose of any proceedings of the Court, shall while absent from the Centre be kept in the custody of the officer designated in that behalf by the Warden.

(2) An appellant when absent from the Centre under this Rule shall wear his own clothing or, if his own clothing cannot be used, clothing different from Centre dress.

Payments

87. If an appellant is ordered to be released by the Court of Criminal Appeal otherwise than on bail pending the hearing of his appeal, payments related to his industry at a rate fixed by the Commissioners shall be made to him in respect of the time during which he has been treated as subject to this section of these Rules.

Private medical adviser and other visitors

88.—(1) An appellant may for the purposes of his appeal receive a visit from a registered medical practitioner selected by him or by his friends or legal adviser, under the same conditions as apply to a visit by his legal adviser.

(2) An appellant may for the purposes of his appeal receive a visit from any other person.

Letters and other facilities

89.—(1) Writing materials to such extent as the Warden considers reasonable shall be furnished to any appellant who requires them for the purpose of preparing his appeal.

(2) An appellant may write letters to his legal adviser or other persons for the purpose of his appeal.

(3) A confidential written communication prepared as instructions for the legal adviser of an appellant may be delivered personally to such legal adviser, without being examined by an officer, unless the Warden has reason to suppose that it contains matter not relating to such instructions, but all other written communications shall be treated as letters, and shall not be sent out without being previously inspected by the Warden.

The Detention Centre Rules

General obligations

90.—(1) Every officer shall conform to these Rules and to the regulations of the Centre and shall support the Warden in the maintenance thereof.

(2) Every officer shall obey the lawful instructions of the Warden.

(3) Every officer shall at once communicate to the Warden any abuses or impropriety which may come to his knowledge.

Sick inmates

91. Every officer shall direct the attention of the Warden to any inmate (whether he complains or not) who appears to be out of health or whose state of mind appears to be deserving of special notice and care, and the Warden shall without delay bring such cases to the notice of the Medical Officer.

Business transactions

92.—(1) No officer shall without the authority of the Commissioners carry out any pecuniary or business transactions with or on behalf of an inmate.

(2) No officer shall without authority bring in or carry out, or attempt to bring in or carry out, or knowingly allow to be brought in or carried out, to or for an inmate, or deposit in any place with intent that it shall come into possession of an inmate, any article whatsoever.

Gratuities

93. No officer shall receive any unauthorized fee, gratuity, or other consideration in connexion with his duty.

Ex-inmates, etc.

94. No officer shall knowingly communicate with an ex-inmate or with the friends or relatives of an inmate or ex-inmate except with the knowledge of the Warden.

Search if required

95. Every officer shall submit himself to be searched in the Centre if called upon to do so by the Warden.

Communications to press, etc.

96.—(1) No officer shall, directly or indirectly, make any unauthorized communication to representatives of the press or other persons in reference to matters which have become known to him in the course of his duty.

(2) No officer shall without authority publish any matter or make any public pronouncement relating to the administration or the inmates of an institution to which the Prison Acts, 1865 to 1898, apply.

Quarters

97.—(1) Every officer shall occupy such quarters as may be assigned to him and shall at any time vacate them if required to do so.

(2) On the termination of an officer's service he shall give up the quarters he has occupied as soon as he is required to do so; and on the death of an officer his family shall give up the quarters when required to do so.

Code of discipline

98. A code of discipline, setting out the offences against discipline, the procedure for dealing therewith, and the awards therefor, shall be formulated by the Commissioners with the approval of the Secretary of State and shall apply to such classes of officers as are stated in the code.

BOARDS OF VISITORS

Term of office

99. The members of a Board of Visitors appointed by the Secretary of State under subsection (2) of section fifty-three of the Criminal Justice Act, 1948(**f**), shall hold office for such a period, not exceeding three years, as he may fix.

Chairman

100.—(1) When a Board of Visitors is initially constituted one of the members shall be appointed by the Secretary of State to be chairman for a period of twelve months.

(2) Except as provided by the foregoing paragraph the Board of Visitors shall at their first meeting in each year of office appoint a chairman and shall, if a casual vacancy occurs in the office of chairman, fill the vacancy as soon as possible.

Meetings and visits

101. The Board shall meet at the Centre at least once a month to discharge their functions under these Rules, and members of the Board shall frequently visit and inspect the Centre.

Rota and quorum

102.—(1) The Board shall at their first meeting arrange a rota of attendance at the Centre and fix a quorum not less than three for the purpose of carrying out their duties, and may at that or a later meeting appoint a vice-chairman, who, unless upon the occurrence of a casual vacancy in the office of chairman he is himself appointed chairman, shall hold office during the term of office for which the chairman has been appointed.

(2) The quorum fixed in pursuance of the foregoing paragraph shall not be required for performing a function which in accordance with an express provision of these Rules may be performed by a smaller number.

Vacancies

103. The powers of the Board shall not be affected by vacancies, so long as the quorum for meetings is sufficient.

Minutes

104. The Board shall keep minutes of their proceedings.

Inquiries, etc.

105. The Board shall co-operate with the Commissioners and with the Warden in promoting the efficiency of the Centre, and shall make inquiry into any matter specially referred to the Board by the Secretary of State or the Commissioners, and report thereon.

The Detention Centre Rules

Abuses

106. The Board shall bring all abuses in connexion with the Centre which come to their knowledge to the notice of the Commissioners immediately, and in case of urgent necessity may suspend an officer until the decision of the Commissioners is made known.

Adjudication, report, etc.

107.—(1) The Board shall hear and adjudicate on such offences as under Rule 33 are referred to them.

(2) They shall furnish such information with respect to the offences reported to them and their awards as may from time to time be required by the Commissioners or the Secretary of State.

Access to Centre

108.—(1) The Board and all members of the Board shall have free access to all parts of the Centre and to all inmates, and may see such inmates as they desire, out of sight and hearing of officers.

(2) They shall hear and investigate any application which an inmate desires to make to them, and if necessary shall report the same, with their opinion to the Commissioners.

Sick inmates

109. The Board shall attend to any report which they receive that the mind or body of an inmate is likely to be injured by the conditions of his detention, and shall communicate their opinion to the Commissioners. If the case is urgent, they shall give such directions thereon as they deem expedient, communicating the same to the Commissioners.

Restraint

110. If the Warden represents to a member of the Board that he or the Medical Officer has, in pursuance of the provisions of these Rules in that behalf, put an inmate under mechanical restraint, and that it is necessary that the inmate be so kept for more than twenty-four hours, such member may authorize the continuance of that restraint by order in writing, which shall specify the cause thereof and the time during which the inmate is to be so kept.

Diet

111. The Board shall inspect the dietary of inmates and if they find the quality of the food unsatisfactory they shall report the matter to the Commissioners and note the same in their minutes, and the Warden shall immediately take such steps thereupon as may be necessary.

Books

112. The Board may inspect any of the books of the Centre, and a note of any such inspection shall be made in their minutes.

Additional visits or letters

113. The Board may, in any case of special importance or urgency, allow an inmate an additional visit or letter.

Denominational records

114. The Board shall investigate and decide on every application from an inmate to change the record of his religious denomination. Before granting such an application, they shall satisfy themselves that it is made from conscientious motives, and not from caprice or a desire to escape any regulations of the Centre.

Buildings

115. The Board may inquire into the state of the buildings of the Centre, and if any repairs or additions appear to them to be necessary shall report thereon with their advice and suggestions to the Secretary of State or the Commissioners.

Annual and other reports

116. The Board shall make an annual report at the end of each year to the Secretary of State with regard to all or any of the matters referred to in these Rules, with their advice and suggestions upon any such matter, and they may make such other reports to the Secretary of State or to the Commissioners as they consider necessary concerning any matter relating to the Centre to which, in their opinion, attention should be drawn.

Permissions and consultation

117. The Board shall, before granting any permission which they have power to grant under these Rules, satisfy themselves by consultation with the Warden that it can be granted without interfering with the security, good order, and proper government of the Centre and inmates therein, and if after such permission has been granted its continuance seems likely to cause such interference, or an inmate has abused permission granted to him or has been guilty of misconduct, they may suspend or withdraw the permission.

Contracts

118. A member of a Board of Visitors of a Centre shall not have any interest in any contract made in respect of that Centre.

> *David Maxwell Fyfe,*
> One of Her Majesty's Principal
> Secretaries of State.

Home Office,
Whitehall.
28th July, 1952.

INDEX

accommodation, 4, 13
Advisory Council on Treatment of Offenders, 4, 5
age of offenders, 31, 45, 46, 129
after-care, 3, 6, 11, 137-8
Aldington, Kent, 13, 15
appeal, 48, 49*t*
approved schools, x, 1, 2, 12, 29, 30, 37, 48*t*, 59, 94
schoolboys, 3, 54, 80, 90, 93
army, ix, 59, 71
arrest, 27
association (with other inmates), 17, 62, 113
attendance centres, 1, 2, 4
breach of order, 24, 25, 47
report, 80
senior, xii, 4, 30, 47
attitude research, x
attitudes, xii, 19, 47, 50, 52, 53, 55, 59, 62, 67, 73*t*, 81-83, 94, 115 122, 131

Blantyre House, ix, 3, 4, 11, 13, 18, 19, 51, 69
boredom, 53, 104
borstal, x, 1, 2, 4-7, 9-11, 29, 32, 46, 47, 52-54
girls, 12
British Journal of Delinquency, ix*n*, 3*n*

Campsfield House, ix, 2 *see also* detention centres, junior
Carr-Saunders, 34*n*, 36
cars, hired, 22, 42

stolen, 26, 29, 44 *see also* offences, taking and driving away, disqualified driving and motoring offences
theft of, 22, 23 *see also* (as above)
cells, 13
detention, 20, 53
children's homes, 59
changing, *see* clothes
church, services, 13
cigarettes, 41, 63, *see also* smoking
circuit training, 62, 63, 65*t*, 66, 101, (*and n*), 102*t*
cleanliness, 14, 15, 53
clothes, changing of, 14, 15, 66, 101, 102*t*
expenditure on, 41
clubs *see* leisure
companionship, 42*t*, 44*t*, 59, *see also* friends
corporal punishment, 1, 2, 20, 123
corrective training, 1
court(s), 4, 10, 27, 48*t*, 49*t*, 55
Crown, 51
higher, 27, 47
juvenile, 2, 3
magistrates', 47, 51
midland, 134
northern, 134
criminal, definition of, 116-7
records, 22
criminality, 84, 85, 86, 90, 111, 122, 130
history of, 28, 29, 31, 32, *see also* criminal records, previous offences
activities, 38, 57, 58

Criminal Justice Act, 1948, 1, 4,
24*n*, 27, 31, 134
1961, 6, 137, 139
Bill, 1938, 1
1960, 5, 6

dances and dancing, 24, 41*n*, 42, 51,
98*t*, *see also* leisure
dance-halls, 23, 100*t*
deafness, 24, 46
death sentence, 2
detention centre(s), admission to, 50
'case', 54, 57, *see also* 'type'
junior, ix, 2, 30, 48*t*, 51, 52, 59,
69, 80, 93, 94 *see also* Campsfield
House
rules, 14, 19, 20, Appendix III
deterrence, 3, 5, 133
detterent effect, 138
element, 62
punishment, 55
regime, 6
treatment, 69
discharge, conditional, etc, 30
from detention centre, 18, 71 72,
126, 136, 137, *see also* release,
plans for, 95-97, 99, 137
disciplinary offences, 14, 19*t*
discipline, at detention centre, 12,
63, 70*t*, 71*t*, 72, 102
in home, 36, 123
dishonest activities, 23, 43
dishonesty, offences of, 8*t*, 22, 25*t*
26 (*and t*), 28, 31*t*, 32, 33*t*,
39, 40*t*, 44*t*, 45 (*and t*), 128, *see
also* offenders
breaking and entering, 22, 29, 30
larceny, 2, 30
meterbreaking, 48*t*, 49*t*
receiving, 22, 24
robbery, 22, 44
theft, 26, *see also* car
disorderly behaviour, disorderliness, 2, 24*n*, 30, *see also* drunkenness
disqualified driving, 23, 25*t*, 26 (*and
t*), 31*t*, 33*t*, 39, 40*t*, 44*t*, 45*t*,
77, 93, 100, 121

dormitories, 13, 14, 18
drill, 63, 64*t*, 65*t*, 102*t*
drink, drinking, 18, 23, 24, 25, 29,
30, 41 (*and n*), 59, 98, 99, 100*t*,
134
drunkenness, 2, 10, 18 (*and n*),
23, 24, 25, 29, 43, 47, 48*t*, 70

early rising, 62, 64*t*, 65*t*, 66, 102
(*and t*)
earnings in centre, 19, 20, *for other
earnings see* wages; employment
employers, 32
employment, in centre, 12, 15, 89
domestic, 12, 14, 15
farm, 12, 15
gardens, 12, 15
maintenance, 12, 15
mats, 15
mattresses, 15
painting and decorating, 15
scrubbing, 62, 64*t*, 65*t*, 66, 102*t*,
103, 107
employment outside centre, ix, 38-
40, 134
dismissal from, 89
future (after discharge), 96, 126,
130
habits at, 22
record, 29, 32
skilled, 39
time spent in, 40*t*
unemployment, ix, 97, 134
Youth Employment Office, 137
evening activities & classes, 12, 16,
62*n*, 66, 104-5, 113-114, 135

family, 31, 71, 96 (*and n*), 100*t*, 104,
126, 131, 134
circumstances, 31, 32, 34, 35, 82
cohesion, 34, 36
composition, 32-34
difficulties, 104
history, 22, 32
reaction of to sentence, xi
relationships, ix, 35, 36, 134
size of, 34
ties, 100

father, relationships with, 35, 36, 61, 123, *see also* family
fence, 26
fine, 1, 4, 30, 46, 47, 52, 56, 80, 119*t*
non-payment of, 24, 31
follow-up, xii, 125-32
letter, xii
food, 62, 63 *(and n)* 64*t*, 65*t*, 101 *(and n)*, 102*t*
football *see* physical training; leisure
Ford, Donald, 3*n*
freedom, 15, 99*n*, *see also* liberty
loss of, 98
friends, 36 *(and t)*, 42-4, 59, 71, 96, 98*t*, 99, 100*t*, *see also* companionship and gangs
at centre, 112-3
girl-, 36 *(and t)*, 41, 42 *(and t)*, 59, 71, 96, 98*t*, 99, 100*t*, 114*t*

gang, 43, 44*t*, 59, *see also* friends and companionship
Glueck, Sheldon and Eleanor, 31*n* 32*n*
Goudhurst (*see* Blantyre House)
grade, 19, 20, 111
Grunhut, Max, 3*n*, 5*n*
gymnasium, 12, 13

haircuts, 41, 48*t*, 61
Hansard, 1*n*, 2*n*
home, 99, 100, 114*t*, *see also* family
Home Office, xi, 4, 139
Home Secretary (Chuter-Ede), 1
Howard Houses, 1, 2
residential hostels, 2

illegitimacy, 34, 134
illiteracy, *see* reading
indecent exposure, 24, 29, 112, 116
inspections, kit, 70
institutional experience, 90
treatment, 30, 59, 60, 85, 118
institutions, 35
intelligence, 37-8, 127, *see also* under school
at detention centre, 86-7
dullness, dull, 28, 37, 86, 87

low, xiii
quotient, 24, 29, 37, 38
Ireland, 32, 48*t*, 96

judges, 4, 55

kitchens, 13

labour exchanges, 127
leisure, xi, 22, 42, 100*t*
billiard halls, 42
camping, 42
cinema, 42
dances *see under* dances
football, 42
hobbies, 42
on release, 98
Clubs (Youth etc) 51, 100*t*
-leader, 79
letters, inmates', 108, 109
liberty, 60, 137, *see also* freedom
Liverpool, 32, 51
local authority, care of, 30
London, 32, 38 *(and n)*
greater, 32

McLintock F., 34*n*
magistrates, 4
Magistrates Association, 2, 139
maladjustment, 24, 84
maladjusted children, 37, 46
treatment in mental hospital, 46, 61, 84, 131
malicious damage, 10, 28
Manchester, 32, 51
manners, 77, 83
marching, 62-66, 70, 101, 102*t*
marriage, 34
Mannheim H. and Wilkins L., 31*n*, 32*n*, 37 *(and n)*
Medomsley, 12
mental hospital, *see* maladjustment
merchant navy, 59
money, *see also*, earnings, employ-ment and wages
spending of, 41
motor cycles, 26, 41*n*, 42

motoring offences, 7*t*, 8*t*, 10, 22, 30, 58, 116, 123, *see also* cars, disqualified driving and taking and driving
murder, 58, 116*t*

New Hall (Wakefield), 12
North, 32, 38 (*and n*), 40, 41, 99
Norwood East, 34*n*

offences, *see* dishonesty, offences of, violence, offences of, motoring offences, sexual offences, taking and driving
planning of, 44, 45, 58,
offenders, dishonest, 6, 10, 38, 43, 51, 56, 57, 58, 79, 94, 116, 117, 135, housebreakers, 26, *see also* dishonesty
first, 28, 29, 48*t*, 49*t*, 56, 57, 117
'others', 56
persistent, repeated, 57, 117
take and drive away, 43 *see also under* taking and driving away
violent, 18, 43, 57, 78 *and* 78*n*, 81, 93, 111, 116*t*, 117, 121, 123, 128, *see also under* violence
offensive weapon, 24, 26
officers
prison officers, x
prison officers in detention centres, xi, 13, 14, 16, 17, 18, 20, 54, 60, 61, 67, 75-94, 105-6, 107-10, 135
quarters, 15
remarks of, 122
staff (detention centre)
chaplain, 18
chief officer, 17, 18
deputy warden, 18, 20
house officer, 76
medical officer, 18
medical orderly, 18
night duty officer, 14
physical training officer, 17, 68, 76 (*and n*) 87, 88
principal officer, 17, 18
reception officer, 50, 68

social worker, 137
warden, xi, 17, 18, 20
training, 17*n*
treatment by, 64*t*, 65*t*, 68, 102*t*
order, *see also* under sentence
breach of, 55
length of, 6, 18, 46 *and t*, 47, 48*t*, 49*t*, 80, 92

parade, 15, 62, 63, 64*t*, 65*t*, 102*t*
Parliament, 1 *and n*, 2 (House of Lords), 5
Penal Practice in a Changing Society, xi, 5 (*and n*), 11*n*
perimeter wire, 12, 13, 20
personal relationships, 14, 89, 91
Perth (detention centre) xii
physical condition, 46, 87
physical training, 14, 62, 63, 66, 70, 72, 87, 88 (*and t*) 101*n* and 102*t*
instructor, *see* officers
football, 17
rugby, 17
playing fields, 12
police, 23, 27, 96, 124
popularity, 89, 90, 91, 113
prediction (by officers), 92, 93 (*and t*)
previous court appearances, 31
previous convictions, 9*t*, 10, 27, 28, 29, 30, 85, 93, 129*t*, 135
Prison Commission, ix, x, 2, 4, 46 (Reports of), 3 (*and n*), 6*n*, 10*n*, 11*n*, 12*n*, 15*n*, 19*n*, 20*n*
prison, x, 1, 2, 4, 5, 6, 7*t*, 8*t*, 9*t*, 10, 11, 16, 27, 28*n*, 31, 46, 51, 52, 53, 56, 60, 66, 73, 118, 119*t*, 131
programme (daily) 62, 66, 67, 69, 102*t*
privileges, 19, 53, 59
(in borstal) 54
probation, 54-56, 73, 119*t*
order, 1, 29, 30, 52
officer, xii, 3, 107, 137
records of, 32
psychiatric report, 24
psychologist (prison) 61*n*

punishment, x, 2, 17, 24, 51, 52, 55, 56, 57, 104, 117, 123-4
  within detention centres, 18, 19, 20, 73, 75, 80, 107-110

race,
  fighting, 23*n*, 48, 49*t*
  prejudice, 91, 113
radio, 17
rape, 24, 58, 112, 116
reading, 15, 104
  lessons, 16
  illiteracy, 37
recidivism, attitude to, 122
reconvictions, ix, x, 3, 10, 11, 29, 35, 81, 86, 127-131
records (gramophone) 17, 41*n*, 42
Registrar General's Statistical Review, 34
release, 11, *see also* discharge
remand
  (bail), 27
  (custody), 27
Remand Centres, 4
remission, forfeiture of, 19, 20, 109

school, *see also* intelligence
  education, 14
  educationally subnormal, 24, 86
  family size in relation to education, 32
  habits at, 22
  records at, 29, 32, 37, 80, 87
  truancy, 29, 37, 48*t*
  type of,
    E.S.N., 37*t*, 86, 134
    grammar, 36, 37*t*, 39
    residential, 36, 37*t*
    secondary modern, 36, 37*t*
    technical, 36, 37*t*, 39
Scottish Advisory Council, 6 (*and n*)
security, 12, 13
sentence, *see also* order
  attitude to, 50, 117-120, 127
  detention centre, 56, 60

length of, 4-6, 8, 10, 54, 111, 113, 130, 138-9
policy, 10
severity of, 52
sexual offences, 8*t*, 22, 58, 79, 90, *see also under* rape and indecent exposure
Sheffield, 32
short-term institutions, 4
short-term treatment, 29, 60
showers, 13
smoking, 41, 53, 59, 64*t*, 65*t*, 98*t*, 99, 102*t*, *see also under* cigarettes
South, 40
Southwest, 99
Staff (detention centre), *see* officers
supervision, 12, 15, 17, 114
  probationary, 55, 131
suspect person, 24, 27, 115*n*
swimming pool, 12

taken into consideration, 22, 28*n*, 49*t*
taking and driving away (of cars), 8*t*, 22, 23, 25*t*, 26*t*, 28, 30, 31*t*, 33*t*, 40*t*, 41, 43, 44*t*, 45 (*and t*), 48*t*, 58, 78 (*and n*) 81, 86, 93, 99, 116*t*, 134
television, 42, 53
Templewood (Lord) (Sir Samuel Hoare), 2
training
  borstal, 6
  detention centre, 12
  methods, 11
  officers assessments of behaviour in, 76-94
  results of, 91, 92
  trade, 53
trial, 27
type,
  detention centre type, 57, 83, 84, 85, 134
  violent type, 37
  see also detention centre

victimization, 27

violence, offences of, 7*t*, 8*t*, 10*t*, 22,
    25 (*and t*), 26 (*and t*), 28, 31, 33*t*,
    39, 40*t*, 41, 44*t*, 45 (*and t*), 48*t*,
    57, 61, 99, 116*t*, 134
  affray, 48*t*, 116
  assault, 8*t*, 23, 29, 54, 70, 79
  assault on police, 23
  grievous bodily harm, 8*t*, 58
visits, 18, 52

wages, 39, 40, 41, *see also* earnings
  and employment

spending of, 41
warden, *see* officers
weekends, 16, 100*t*
wilful damage, 2, 10, 24
Wilkins L., 34*n*
Wormwood Scrubs, 27, 51

Young Prisoners' Centre, 11, 12, 13
Youth Service in England and
  Wales (Report of), 41*n*

The International Library of
Sociology
and Social Reconstruction

Edited by W. J. H. SPROTT
Founded by KARL MANNHEIM

ROUTLEDGE & KEGAN PAUL
BROADWAY HOUSE, CARTER LANE, LONDON, E.C.4

CONTENTS

General Sociology	3
Foreign Classics of Sociology	3
Social Structure	4
Sociology and Politics	4
Foreign Affairs, Their Social, Political and Economic Foundations	5
Sociology of Law	5
Criminology	5
Social Psychology	6
Sociology of the Family	7
The Social Services	7
Sociology of Education	8
Sociology of Culture	9
Sociology of Religion	9
Sociology of Art and Literature	9
Sociology of Knowledge	9
Urban Sociology	10
Rural Sociology	10
Sociology of Migration	11
Sociology of Industry and Distribution	11
Anthropology	12
Documentary	13
Reports of the Institute of Community Studies	14

PRINTED IN GREAT BRITAIN BY HEADLEY BROTHERS LTD
109 KINGSWAY LONDON WC2 AND ASHFORD KENT

GENERAL SOCIOLOGY

Brown, Robert. Explanation in Social Science. *208 pp. 1963. (2nd Impression 1964.) 25s.*

Gibson, Quentin. The Logic of Social Enquiry. *240 pp. 1960. (2nd Impression 1963.) 24s.*

Goldschmidt, Professor Walter. Understanding Human Society. *272 pp. 1959. 21s.*

Homans, George C. Sentiments and Activities: Essays in Social Science. *336 pp. 1962. 32s.*

Jarvie, I. C. The Revolution in Anthropology. *Foreword by Ernest Gellner. 272 pp. 1964. 40s.*

Johnson, Harry M. Sociology: a Systematic Introduction. *Foreword by Robert K. Merton. 710 pp. 1961. (4th Impression 1964.) 42s.*

Mannheim, Karl. Essays on Sociology and Social Psychology. *Edited by Paul Keckskemeti. With Editorial Note by Adolph Lowe. 344 pp. 1953. 30s.*

Systematic Sociology: An Introduction to the Study of Society. *Edited by J. S. Erös and Professor W. A. C. Stewart. 220 pp. 1957. (2nd Impression 1959.) 24s.*

Martindale, Don. The Nature and Types of Sociological Theory. *292 pp. 1961. 35s.*

Maus, Heinz. A Short History of Sociology. *234 pp. 1962. 28s.*

Myrdal, Gunnar. Value in Social Theory: A Collection of Essays on Methodology. *Edited by Paul Streeten. 332 pp. 1958. (2nd Impression 1962.) 32s.*

Ogburn, William F., and **Nimkoff, Meyer F.** A Handbook of Sociology. *Preface by Karl Mannheim. 656 pp. 46 figures. 38 tables. 5th edition (revised) 1964. 40s.*

Parsons, Talcott and **Smelser, Neil J.** Economy and Society: A Study in the Integration of Economic and Social Theory. *362 pp. 1956. (3rd Impression 1964.) 35s.*

Rex, John. Key Problems of Sociological Theory. *220 pp. 1961. (2nd Impression 1963.) 25s.*

Stark, Werner. The Fundamental Forms of Social Thought. *280 pp. 1962. 32s.*

FOREIGN CLASSICS OF SOCIOLOGY

Durkheim, Emile. Suicide. A Study in Sociology. *Edited and with an Introduction by George Simpson. 404 pp. 1952. (2nd Impression 1963.) 30s.*

Socialism and Saint-Simon. *Edited with an Introduction by Alvin W. Gouldner. Translated by Charlotte Sattler from the edition originally edited with an Introduction by Marcel Mauss. 286 pp. 1959. 28s.*

Professional Ethics and Civic Morals. *Translated by Cornelia Brookfield. 288 pp. 1957. 30s.*

Gerth, H. H., and **Wright Mills, C.** From Max Weber: Essays in Sociology. *502 pp. 1948. (5th Impression 1964.) 35s.*

Tönnies, Ferdinand. Community and Association. *(Gemeinschaft und Gesellschaft.) Translated and Supplemented by Charles P. Loomis. Foreword by Pitirim A. Sorokin. 334 pp. 1955. 28s.*

3

SOCIAL STRUCTURE

Andrzejewski, Stanislaw. Military Organization and Society. *With a Foreword by Professor A. R. Radcliffe-Brown. 226 pp. 1 folder. 1954. 21s.*

Cole, G. D. H. Studies in Class Structure. *220 pp. 1955. (3rd Impression 1964.) 21s.*

Coontz, Sydney H. Population Theories and the Economic Interpretation. *202 pp. 1957. (2nd Impression 1961.) 25s.*

Coser, Lewis. The Functions of Social Conflict. *204 pp. 1956. 18s.*

Glass, D. V. (Ed.). Social Mobility in Britain. *Contributions by J. Berent, T. Bottomore, R. C. Chambers, J. Floud, D. V. Glass, J. R. Hall, H. T. Himmelweit, R. K. Kelsall, F. M. Martin, C. A. Moser, R. Mukherjee, and W. Ziegel. 420 pp. 1954. (2nd Impressions 1963.) 40s.*

Kelsall, R. K. Higher Civil Servants in Britain: From 1870 to the Present Day. *268 pp. 31 tables. 1955. 25s.*

Ossowski, Stanislaw. Class Structure in the Social Consciousness. *212 pp. 1963. 25s.*

SOCIOLOGY AND POLITICS

Barbu, Zevedei. Democracy and Dictatorship: Their Psychology and Patterns of Life. *300 pp. 1956. 28s.*

Benney, Mark, Gray, A. P., and Pear, R. H. How People Vote: a Study of Electoral Behaviour in Greenwich. *Foreword by Professor W. A. Robson. 256 pp. 70 tables. 1956. 25s.*

Bramstedt, Dr. E. K. Dictatorship and Political Police: The Technique of Control by Fear. *286 pp. 1945. 20s.*

Crick, Bernard. The American Science of Politics: Its Origins and Conditions. *284 pp. 1959. 28s.*

Hertz, Frederick. Nationality in History and Politics: A Psychology and Sociology of National Sentiment and Nationalism. *440 pp. 1944. (4th Impression 1957.) 32s.*

Kornhauser, William. The Politics of Mass Society. *272 pp. 20 tables. 1960. 25s.*

Laidler, Harry W. Social-Economic Movements: An Historical and Comparative Survey of Socialism, Communism, Co-operation, Utopianism; and other Systems of Reform and Reconstruction. *864 pp. 16 plates. 1 figure. 1949. (3rd Impression 1960.) 50s.*

Mannheim, Karl. Freedom, Power and Democratic Planning. *Edited by Hans Gerth and Ernest K. Bramstedt. 424 pp. 1951. 35s.*

Mansur, Fatma. Process of Independence. *Foreword by A. H. Hanson. 208 pp. 1962. 25s.*

Myrdal, Gunnar. The Political Element in the Development of Economic Theory. *Translated from the German by Paul Streeten. 282 pp. 1953. (3rd Impression 1961.) 25s.*

Polanyi, Michael, F.R.S. The Logic of Liberty: Reflections and Rejoinders. *228 pp. 1951. 18s.*

Verney, Douglas V. The Analysis of Political Systems. *264 pp. 1959. (2nd Impression 1961.) 28s.*

Wootton, Graham. The Politics of Influence: British Ex-Servicemen, Cabinet Decisions and Cultural Changes, 1917 to 1957. *320 pp. 1963. 30s.*

FOREIGN AFFAIRS: THEIR SOCIAL, POLITICAL AND ECONOMIC FOUNDATIONS

Baer, Gabriel. Population and Society in the Arab East. *Translated by Hanna Szöke. 288 pp. 10 maps. 1964. 40s.*

Bonné, Alfred. The Economic Development of the Middle East: An Outline of Planned Reconstruction after the War. *192 pp. 58 tables. 1945. (3rd Impression 1953.) 16s.*
State and Economics in the Middle East: A Society in Transition. *482 pp. 2nd (revised) edition 1955. (2nd Impression 1960.) 40s.*
Studies in Economic Development: with special reference to Conditions in the Under-developed Areas of Western Asia and India. *322 pp. 84 tables. (2nd edition 1960.) 32s.*

Mayer, J. P. Political Thought in France from the Revolution to the Fifth Republic. *164 pp. 3rd edition (revised) 1961. 16s.*

Schlesinger, Rudolf. Central European Democracy and its Background: Economic and Political Group Organization. *432 pp. 1953. 40s.*

Thomson, David, Meyer, E., and Briggs, A. Patterns of Peacemaking. *408 pp. 1945. 25s.*

Trouton, Ruth. Peasant Renaissance in Yugoslavia, 1900-1950: A Study of the Development of Yugoslav Peasant Society as affected by Education. *370 pp. 1 map. 1952. 28s.*

SOCIOLOGY OF LAW

Gurvitch, Dr. Georges. Sociology of Law. *With a Preface by Professor Roscoe Pound. 280 pp. 1947. (2nd Impression 1953.) 24s.*

Renner, Karl. The Institutions of Private Law and Their Social Functions. *Edited, with an Introduction and Notes by O. Kahn-Freund. Translated by Agnes Schwarzschild. 336 pp. 1949. 28s.*

CRIMINOLOGY

Cloward, Richard A., and Ohlin, Lloyd E. Delinquency and Opportunity: A Theory of Delinquent Gangs. *248 pp. 1961. 25s.*

Friedländer, Dr. Kate. The Psycho-Analytical Approach to Juvenile Delinquency: Theory, Case Studies, Treatment. *320 pp. 1947. (5th Impression 1961.) 28s.*

Glueck, Sheldon and Eleanor. Family Environment and Delinquency. *With the statistical assistance of Rose W. Kneznek. 340 pp. 1962. 35s.*

Mannheim, Hermann. Group Problems in Crime and Punishment, and other Studies in Criminology and Criminal Law. *336 pp. 1955. 28s.*

Morris, Terence. The Criminal Area: A Study in Social Ecology. *Foreword by Hermann Mannheim. 232 pp. 25 tables. 4 maps. 1957. 25s.*

Morris, Terence and **Pauline,** assisted by **Barbara Barer.** Pentonville: a Sociological Study of an English Prison. *416 pp. 16 plates. 1963. 50s.*

Spencer, John C. Crime and the Services. *Foreword by Hermann Mannheim. 336 pp. 1954. 28s.*

Trasler, Gordon. The Explanation of Criminality. *144 pp. 1962. 20s.*

SOCIAL PSYCHOLOGY

Barbu, Zevedei. Problems of Historical Psychology. *248 pp. 1960. 25s.*

Blackburn, Julian. Psychology and the Social Pattern. *184 pp. 1945. (6th Impression 1961.) 16s.*

Fleming, C. M. Adolescence: Its Social Psychology: With an Introduction to recent findings from the fields of Anthropology, Physiology, Medicine, Psychometrics and Sociometry. *271 pp. 2nd edition (revised) 1963. (2nd impression 1964) 25s.*
The Social Psychology of Education: An Introduction and Guide to Its Study. *136 pp. 2nd edition (revised) 1959. 11s.*

Fleming, C. M. (Ed.). Studies in the Social Psychology of Adolescence. *Contributions by J. E. Richardson, J. F. Forrester, J. K. Shukla and P. J. Higginbotham. Foreword by the editor. 292 pp. 29 figures. 13 tables. 5 folder tables. 1951. 23s.*

Halmos, Paul. Solitude and Privacy: a Study of Social Isolation, its Causes and Therapy. *With a Foreword by Professor T. H. Marshall. 216 pp. 1952. 21s.*
Towards a Measure of Man: The Frontiers of Normal Adjustment. *276 pp. 1957. 28s.*

Homans, George C. The Human Group. *Foreword by Bernard DeVoto. Introduction by Robert K. Merton. 526 pp. 1951. (4th Impression 1963.) 35s.*
Social Behaviour: its Elementary Forms. *416 pp. 1961. 30s.*

Klein, Josephine. The Study of Groups. *226 pp. 31 figures. 5 tables. 1956. (3rd Impression 1962.) 21s.*

Linton, Ralph. The Cultural Background of Personality. *132 pp. 1947. (5th Impression 1964.) 16s.*
See also Yang, M.

Mayo, Elton. The Social Problems of an Industrial Civilization. With an appendix on the Political Problem. *180 pp. 1949. (4th Impression 1961.) 18s.*

Ridder, J. C. de. The Personality of the Urban African in South Africa. A Thematic Apperception Test Study. *196 pp. 12 plates. 1961. 25s.*

Rose, Arnold M. (Ed.). Mental Health and Mental Disorder: A Sociological Approach. *Chapters by 46 contributors. 654 pp. 1956. 45s.*
Human Behavior and Social Processes: an Interactionist Approach. *Contributions by Arnold M. Ross, Ralph H. Turner, Anselm Strauss, Everett C. Hughes, E. Franklin Frazier, Howard S. Becker, et al. 696 pp. 1962. 60s.*

Smelser, Neil J. Theory of Collective Behavior. *448 pp. 1962. 45s.*

Spinley, Dr. B. M. The Deprived and the Privileged: Personality Development in English Society. *232 pp. 1953. 20s.*

Wolfenstein, Martha. Disaster: A Psychological Essay. *264 pp. 1957. 23s.*

Young, Professor Kimball. Personality and Problems of Adjustment. *742 pp. 12 figures. 9 tables. 2nd edition (revised) 1952. (2nd Impression 1959.) 40s.*
Handbook of Social Psychology. *658 pp. 16 figures. 10 tables. 2nd edition (revised) 1957. (3rd Impression 1963.) 40s.*

SOCIOLOGY OF THE FAMILY

Banks, J. A. Prosperity and Parenthood: A Study of Family Planning among the Victorian Middle Classes. *262 pp. 1954. 24s.*

Chapman, Dennis. The Home and Social Status. *336 pp. 8 plates. 3 figures. 117 tables. 1955. 35s.*

Klein, Viola. The Feminine Character: History of an Ideology. *With a Foreword by Karl Mannheim. 256 pp. 1946. 16s.*

Myrdal, Alva and Klein, Viola. Women's Two Roles: Home and Work. *238 pp. 27 tables. 1956. (2nd Impression 1962.) 25s.*

Parsons, Talcott and Bales, Robert F. Family: Socialization and Interaction Process. *In collaboration with James Olds, Morris Zelditch and Philip E. Slater. 456 pp. 50 figures and tables. 1956. 35s.*

THE SOCIAL SERVICES

Ashdown, Margaret and Brown, S. Clement. Social Service and Mental Health: An Essay on Psychiatric Social Workers. *280 pp. 1953. 21s.*

Hall, M. Penelope. The Social Services of Modern England. *416 pp. 6th edition (revised) 1963. 28s.*

Heywood, Jean S. Children in Care: the Development of the Service for the Deprived Child. *256 pp. 1959. (2nd Impression 1964.) 25s.*
An Introduction to teaching Casework Skills. *192 pp. 1964. 28s.*

Jones, Kathleen. Lunacy, Law and Conscience, 1744-1845: the Social History of the Care of the Insane. *268 pp. 1955. 25s.*
Mental Health and Social Policy, 1845-1959. *264 pp. 1960. 28s.*

Jones, Kathleen and Sidebotham, Roy. Mental Hospitals at Work. *220 pp. 1962. 30s.*

Kastell, Jean. Casework in Child Care. *Foreword by M. Brooke Willis. 320 pp. 1962. 35s.*

Rooff, Madeline. Voluntary Societies and Social Policy. *350 pp. 15 tables. 1957. 35s.*

Shenfield, B. E. Social Policies for Old Age: A Review of Social Provision for Old Age in Great Britain. *260 pp. 39 tables. 1957. 25s.*

Timms, Noel. Psychiatric Social Work in Great Britain (1939-1962). *280 pp. 1964. 32s.*
Social Casework: Principles and Practice. *256 pp. 1964, 25s.*

Trasler, Gordon. In Place of Parents: A Study in Foster Care. *272 pp. 1960. 25s.*

Young, A. F., and **Ashton, E. T.** British Social Work in the Nineteenth Century. *288 pp. 1956. (2nd Impression 1963.) 28s.*

SOCIOLOGY OF EDUCATION

Banks, Olive. Parity and Prestige in English Secondary Education: a Study in Educational Sociology. *272 pp. 1955. (2nd Impression. 1963.) 28s.*

Collier, K. G. The Social Purposes of Education: Personal and Social Values in Education. *268 pp. 1959. (2nd Impression 1962.) 21s.*

Edmonds, E. L. The School Inspector. *Foreword by Sir William Alexander. 214 pp. 1962. 28s.*

Evans, K. M. Sociometry and Education. *158 pp. 1962. 18s.*

Fraser, W. R. Education and Society in Modern France. *150 pp. 1963. 20s.*

Hans, Nicholas. New Trends in Education in the Eighteenth Century. *278 pp. 19 tables. 1951. 25s.*
Comparative Education: A Study of Educational Factors and Traditions. *360 pp. 3rd (revised) edition 1958. (4th Impression 1964.) 25s.*

Mannheim, Karl and **Stewart, W. A. C.** An Introduction to the Sociology of Education. *208 pp. 1962. 21s.*

Musgrove, F. Youth and the Social Order. *176 pp. 1964. 21s.*

Ortega y Gasset, Jose. Mission of the University. *Translated with an Introduction by Howard Lee Nostrand. 88 pp. 1946. (3rd Impression 1963.) 15s.*

Ottaway, A. K. C. Education and Society: An Introduction to the Sociology of Education. *With an Introduction by W. O. Lester Smith. 212 pp. Second edition (revised). 1962. (2nd Impression 1964.) 18s.*

Peers, Robert. Adult Education: A Comparative Study. *398 pp. 2nd edition 1959. 35s.*

Pritchard, D. G. Education and the Handicapped: 1760 to 1960. *258 pp. 1963. 28s.*

Samuel, R. H., and **Thomas, R. Hinton.** Education and Society in Modern Germany. *212 pp. 1949. 16s.*

Simon, Brian and **Joan** (Eds.). Educational Psychology in the U.S.S.R. *Introduction by Brian and Joan Simon. Translation by Joan Simon. Papers by D. N. Bogoiavlenski and N. A. Menchinskaia, D. B. Elkonin, E. A. Fleshner, Z. I. Kalmykova, G. S. Kostiuk, V. A. Krutetski, A. N. Leontiev, A. R. Luria, E. A. Milerian, R. G. Natadze, B. M. Teplov, L. S. Vygotski, L. V. Zankov. 296 pp. 1963. 40s.*

SOCIOLOGY OF CULTURE

Fromm, Erich. The Fear of Freedom. *286 pp. 1942. (8th Impression 1960.) 21s.* The Sane Society. *400 pp. 1956. (3rd Impression 1963.) 28s.*

Mannheim, Karl. Diagnosis of Our Time: Wartime Essays of a Sociologist. *208 pp. 1943. (7th Impression 1962.) 21s.*
Essays on the Sociology of Culture. *Edited by Ernst Mannheim in co-operation with Paul Kecskemeti. Editorial Note by Adolph Lowe. 280 pp. 1956. (2nd Impression 1962.) 28s.*

Weber, Alfred. Farewell to European History: or The Conquest of Nihilism. *Translated from the German by R. F. C. Hull. 224 pp. 1947. 18s.*

SOCIOLOGY OF RELIGION

Argyle, Michael. Religious Behaviour. *224 pp. 8 figures. 41 tables. 1958. 25s.*

Knight, Frank H., and **Merriam, Thornton W.** The Economic Order and Religion. *242 pp. 1947. 18s.*

Watt, W. Montgomery. Islam and the Integration of Society. *320 pp. 1961. (2nd Impression.) 32s.*

SOCIOLOGY OF ART AND LITERATURE

Beljame, Alexandre. Men of Letters and the English Public in the Eighteenth Century: 1660-1744, Dryden, Addison, Pope. *Edited with an Introduction and Notes by Bonamy Dobree. Translated by E. O. Lorimer. 532 pp. 1948. 32s.*

Misch, Georg. A History of Autobiography in Antiquity. *Translated by E. W. Dickes. 2 Volumes. Vol. 1, 364 pp., Vol. 2, 372 pp. 1950. 45s. the set.*

Silbermann, Alphons. The Sociology of Music. *224 pp. 1963. 28s.*

SOCIOLOGY OF KNOWLEDGE

Hodges, H. A. The Philosophy of Wilhelm Dilthey. *410 pp. 1952. 30s.*

Mannheim, Karl. Essays on the Sociology of Knowledge. *Edited by Paul Kecskemeti. Editorial note by Adolph Lowe. 352 pp. 1952. (3rd Impression 1964.) 35s.*

Schlesinger, Rudolf. Marx: His Time and Ours. *464 pp. 1950. (2nd Impression 1951.) 32s.*

Stark, W. The History of Economics in its Relation to Social Development. *104 pp. 1944. (4th Impression 1957.) 12s.*

America: Ideal and Reality. The United States of 1776 in Contemporary Philosophy. *136 pp. 1947. 12s.*

The Sociology of Knowledge: An Essay in Aid of a Deeper Understanding of the History of Ideas. *384 pp. 1958. (2nd Impression 1960.) 36s.*

Montesquieu: Pioneer of the Sociology of Knowledge. *244 pp. 1960. 25s.*

URBAN SOCIOLOGY

Anderson, Nels. The Urban Community: A World Perspective. *532 pp. 1960. 35s.*

Ashworth, William. The Genesis of Modern British Town Planning: A Study in Economic and Social History of the Nineteenth and Twentieth Centuries. *288 pp. 1954. 25s.*

Bracey, Howard. Neighbours: Neighbouring and Neighbourliness on New Estates and Subdivisions in England and the U.S.A. *220 pp. 1964. 28s.*

Cullingworth, J. B. Housing Needs and Planning Policy: A Restatement of the Problems of Housing Need and "Overspill" in England and Wales. *232 pp. 44 tables. 8 maps. 1960. 28s.*

Dickinson, Robert E. City and Region: A Geographical Interpretation. *608 pp. 125 figures. 1964. 60s.*

The West European City: A Geographical Interpretation. *600 pp. 129 maps. 29 plates. 2nd edition 1962. (2nd Impression 1963.) 55s.*

Dore, R. P. City Life in Japan: A Study of a Tokyo Ward. *498 pp. 8 plates. 4 figures. 24 tables. 1958. (2nd Impression 1963.) 45s.*

Jennings, Hilda. Societies in the Making: a Study of Development and Redevelopment within a County Borough. *Foreword by D. A. Clark. 286 pp. 1962. 32s.*

Kerr, Madeline. The People of Ship Street. *240 pp. 1958. 23s.*

RURAL SOCIOLOGY

Bracey, H. E. English Rural Life: Village Activities, Organizations and Institutions. *302 pp. 1959. 30s.*

Infield, Henrik F. Co-operative Living in Palestine. *With a Foreword by General Sir Arthur Wauchope, G.C.B. 170 pp. 8 plates. 7 tables. 1946. 12s. 6d.*

Littlejohn, James. Westrigg: the Sociology of a Cheviot Parish. *172 pp. 5 figures. 1963. 25s.*

Saville, John. Rural Depopulation in England and Wales, 1851-1951. *Foreword by Leonard Elmhirst. 286 pp. 6 figures. 39 tables. 1 map. 1957. 28s. (Dartington Hall Studies in Rural Sociology.)*

Williams, W. M. The Country Craftsman: A Study of Some Rural Crafts and the Rural Industries Organization in England. *248 pp. 9 figures. 1958. 25s. (Dartington Hall Studies in Rural Sociology.)*
The Sociology of an English Village: Gosforth. *272 pp. 12 figures. 13 tables. 1956. (3rd Impression 1964.) 25s.*

SOCIOLOGY OF MIGRATION

Eisenstadt, S. N. The Absorption of Immigrants: a Comparative Study based mainly on the Jewish Community in Palestine and the State of Israel. *288 pp. 1954. 28s.*

SOCIOLOGY OF INDUSTRY AND DISTRIBUTION

Anderson, Nels. Work and Leisure. *280 pp. 1961. 28s.*

Blau, Peter M., and **Scott, W. Richard.** Formal Organizations: a Comparative approach. *Introduction and Additional Bibliography by J. H. Smith. 328 pp. 1963. (2nd impression 1964.) 28s.*

Gouldner, Alvin W. Patterns of Industrial Bureaucracy. *298 pp. 1955. 25s.*
Wildcat Strike: A Study of an Unofficial Strike. *202 pp. 10 figures. 1955. 16s.*

Jefferys, Margot, with the assistance of Winifred Moss. Mobility in the Labour Market: Employment Changes in Battersea and Dagenham. *Preface by Barbara Wootton. 186 pp. 51 tables. 1954. 15s.*

Levy, A. B. Private Corporations and Their Control. *Two Volumes. Vol. 1, 464 pp., Vol. 2, 432 pp. 1950. 80s. the set.*

Levy, Hermann. The Shops of Britain: A Study of Retail Distribution. *268 pp. 1948. (2nd Impression 1949.) 21s.*

Liepmann, Kate. The Journey to Work: Its Significance for Industrial and Community Life. *With a Foreword by A. M. Carr-Saunders. 230 pp. 40 tables. 3 folders. 1944. (2nd Impression 1945.) 18s.*
Apprenticeship: An Enquiry into its Adequacy under Modern Conditions. *Foreword by H. D. Dickinson. 232 pp. 6 tables. 1960. (2nd Impression.) 23s.*

Millerson, Geoffrey. The Qualifying Associations: a Study in Professionalization. *320 pp. 1964. 42s.*

Smelser, Neil J. Social Change in the Industrial Revolution: An Application of Theory to the Lancashire Cotton Industry, 1770-1840. *468 pp. 12 figures. 14 tables. 1959. (2nd Impression 1960.) 40s.*

Williams, Gertrude. Recruitment to Skilled Trades. *240 pp. 1957. 23s.*

Young, A. F. Industrial Injuries Insurance: an Examination of British Policy. *192 pp. 1964. 30s.*

ANTHROPOLOGY
(*Demy 8vo.*)

Crook, David and **Isabel.** Revolution in a Chinese Village: Ten Mile Inn. *230 pp. 8 plates. 1 map. 1959. 21s.*

Dube, S. C. Indian Village, *Foreword by Morris Edward Opler. 276 pp. 4 plates. 1955. (4th Impression 1961.) 25s.*
India's Changing Villages: Human Factors in Community Development. *260 pp. 8 plates. 1 map. 1958. (2nd Impression 1960.) 25s.*

Fei, Hsiao-Tung. Peasant Life in China: a Field Study of Country Life in the Yangtze Valley. *Foreword by Bronislaw Malinowski. 320 pp. 14 plates. 1939. (5th Impression 1962.) 30s.*

Gulliver, P. H. The Family Herds. A Study of Two Pastoral Tribes in East Africa, The Jie and Turkana. *304 pp. 4 plates. 19 figures. 1955. 25s.*
Social Control in an African Society: a Study of the Arusha, Agricultural Masai of Northern Tanganyika. *320 pp. 8 plates. 10 figures. 1963. 35s.*

Hogbin, Ian. Transformation Scene. The Changing Culture of a New Guinea Village. *340 pp. 22 plates. 2 maps. 1951. 30s.*

Hsu, Francis L. K. Under the Ancestors' Shadow: Chinese Culture and Personality. *346 pp. 26 figures. 1949. 21s.*

Lowie, Professor Robert H. Social Organization. *494 pp. 1950. (3rd Impression 1962.) 35s.*

Maunier, René. The Sociology of Colonies: An Introduction to the Study of Race Contact. *Edited and translated by E. O. Lorimer. 2 Volumes. Vol. 1, 430 pp., Vol. 2, 356 pp. 1949. 70s. the set.*

Mayer, Adrian C. Caste and Kinship in Central India: A Village and its Region. *328 pp. 16 plates. 15 figures. 16 tables. 1960. 35s.*
Peasants in the Pacific: A Study of Fiji Indian Rural Society. *232 pp. 16 plates. 10 figures. 14 tables. 1961. 35s.*

Osborne, Harold. Indians of the Andes: Aymaras and Quechuas. *292 pp. 8 plates. 2 maps. 1952. 25s.*

Smith, Raymond T. The Negro Family in British Guiana: Family Structure and Social Status in the Villages. *With a Foreword by Meyer Fortes. 314 pp. 8 plates. 1 figure. 4 maps. 1956. 28s.*

Yang, Martin C. A Chinese Village: Taitou, Shantung Province. *Foreword by Ralph Linton. Introduction by M. L. Wilson. 308 pp. 1947. 23s.*

DOCUMENTARY
(*Demy 8vo.*)

Belov, Fedor. The History of a Soviet Collective Farm. *250 pp. 1956. 21s.*

Meek, Dorothea L. (Ed.). Soviet Youth: Some Achievements and Problems. *Excerpts from the Soviet Press, translated by the editor. 280 pp. 1957. 28s.*

Schlesinger, Rudolf (Ed.). Changing Attitudes in Soviet Russia.
1. The Family in the U.S.S.R. *Documents and Readings, with an Introduction by the editor. 434 pp. 1949. 30s.*
2. The Nationalities Problem and Soviet Administration. Selected Readings on the Development of Soviet Nationalities Policies. *Introduced by the editor. Translated by W. W. Gottlieb. 324 pp. 1956. 30s.*

Reports
of the Institute
of Community Studies

(*Demy 8vo.*)

Cartwright, Ann. Human Relations and Hospital Care. *272 pp. 1964. 30s.*

Jackson, Brian and **Marsden, Dennis.** Education and the Working Class: Some General Themes raised by a Study of 88 Working-class Children in a Northern Industrial City. *268 pp. 2 folders. 1962. (2nd Impression.) 28s.*

Marris, Peter. Widows and their Families. *Foreword by Dr. John Bowlby. 184 pp. 18 tables. Statistical Summary. 1958. 18s.*
Family and Social Change in an African City. A Study of Rehousing in Lagos. *196 pp. 1 map. 4 plates. 53 tables. 1961. 25s.*

Mills, Enid. Living with Mental Illness: a Study in East London. *Foreword by Morris Carstairs. 196 pp. 1962. 28s.*

Townsend, Peter. The Family Life of Old People: An Inquiry in East London. *Foreword by J. H. Sheldon. 300 pp. 3 figures. 63 tables. 1957. (2nd Impression 1961.) 30s.*

Willmott, Peter. The Evolution of a Community: a study of Dagenham after forty years. *168 pp. 2 maps. 1963. 21s.*

Willmott, Peter and **Young, Michael.** Family and Class in a London Suburb. *202 pp. 47 tables. 1960. (2nd Impression 1961.) 21s.*

The British Journal of Sociology. *Edited by D. G. MacRae. Vol. 1, No. 1, March 1950 and Quarterly. Roy. 8vo., £2 p.a.; 12s. 6d. a number, post free. (Vols. 1-12, £3 each.)*

All prices are net and subject to alteration without notice